BREAKFASTS..
   ALMOND FRITTATA ....
   HONEY SWEET RAISIN BREAD..10
   VEGAN PUMPKIN COFFEE CAKE OATMEAL................11
   COCOA CHERRY BOWLS...12
   GRANOLA CRUMBLE 13
   MUSHROOM AND SPINACH OMELET PIE.......................14
   BABY SPINACH EGG CUPS 15
   BOILED EGGS WITH SPINACH..17
   COTTAGE CHEESE AND PINE NUT EGG PIE 18
   HAZELNUT AND CHOCOLATE BANANA BREAD..........19
   CREAMY CHICKEN STRIPS 21
   TURKISH BREAKFAST EGGS...22
   COCOA CHERRY BOWLS...23
   MUSHROOM AND CHORIZO MIX 24
   BROCCOLI AND EGGS BREAKFAST......................................25
   SQUASH CINNAMON PORRIDGE..26
   SPINACH FRITTATA..27
   LOADED BREAKFAST POTATOES 28
   BREAKFAST SAUSAGE AND SPINACH FRITTATA 29
   BREAKFAST LOAF...30
VEGETABLES AND VEGAN 32
   CARROTS AND TURNIPS..32
   VEGETARIAN PASTA RECIPE 33
   SLOW COOKED TOMATO CREAM......................................34
   RICED ZUCCHINI WITH CHEESE..35

- LOADED POTATOES 36
- BUTTERNUT DAHL 37
- KETO VEGETABLE CREAM SOUP 38
- EASY SWEET POTATO RECIPE 39
- ZUCCHINI LASAGNA 40
- MUSHROOM SOUP 41
- POTATO AND HERBS 42
- INDIAN COCONUT KALE CURRY 43
- STUFFED BELL PEPPERS 44
- BLACK BEAN SOUP 45
- CHEESY CORN 46
- SUPER-FOOD CASSEROLE 47
- SPICY SWEET POTATO WEDGES 48
- BROCCOLI CAULIFLOWER STIR FRY 49
- SIMPLE EGGPLANT SPREAD 50

SOUPS AND STEWS 52
- CHANAFLOWER MASALA 52
- TACO SOUP 53
- ROSEMARY TURKEY AND KALE SOUP 54
- ASIAN STYLE BROTH 55
- BEEF BORSCHT SOUP 56
- EMERGENCY WHITE CHILI 57
- CORN AND RED PEPPER CHOWDER 58
- SUPER-QUICK CHILI 58
- GINGER CARROT SOUP 59
- BEEF NECK STEW WITH PARMESAN 60
- CHICKEN VEAL STEW 61

- ITALIAN SAUSAGE KALE SOUP...63
- WHOLE CHICKEN AND VEGETABLE STEW..................64
- ETHIOPIAN SPINACH AND LENTIL SOUP......................66
- KOREAN ANCHOVY BROTH...67
- LEMONY FISH BROTH...68
- POMODORO SOUP 70
- HAM AND ASPARAGUS STEW 71
- HOT AND SOUR SOUP 72
- INSTANT POT GOULASH 73

FISH AND SEAFOOD 74
- TROUT WITH BROCCOLI 74
- ADOBO SHRIMPS RECIPE 76
- SIMPLE SALMON 77
- LEMON KALAMATA OLIVE SALMON 78
- CLASSIC SLOW COOKED TUNA NOODLE CASSEROLE 79
- SHRIMP CHOWDER 80
- MAHI MAHI CHILI 81
- ORANGE FISH 82
- CREOLE SHRIMP 84
- KETO SALMON MACARONI...85
- GINGER SQUID 86
- SALMON PATTIES...87
- MEDITERRANEAN-STYLE COD 88
- MISO TROUT 89
- SPICY AND SWEET TROUT 90
- TUNA STEAK WITH MUSHROOMS 91
- EASY CATFISH STEW 93

FISH WITH ORANGE AND GINGER SAUCE 94
CHICKEN AND POULTRY 95
    TURKEY CASSEROLE 95
    TURKEY MEATBALL STEW 96
    DUCK LEGS IN BLACKBERRY SAUCE 97
    CREAMY CHICKEN BACON CHOWDER 98
    TURKEY AND ORANGE SAUCE 99
    ASIAN CHICKEN BOWL 100
    TURKEY AND MUSHROOMS IN A CREAMY WINE SAUCE 101
    ROASTED CHICKEN WITH LEMON AND PARSLEY BUTTER 103
    ONION CHICKEN 104
    MARINARA AND CHEESE STEWED CHICKEN 105
    GREEN CHILI CHICKEN 106
    TANGY CRANBERRY TURKEY 107
    THAI CHICKEN SOUP 108
    FRAGRANT COCONUT CHICKEN 109
    POZOLE BLANCO 111
    BUFFALO CHICKEN SALAD 112
    MARINATED CHICKEN FILLETS 113
    LIME AND SALSA CHICKEN WITH CAULIFLOWER RICE 115
    GROUND TURKEY SOUP 116
    CURRY CHICKEN 117
    COQ AU VIN 119
    JALAPENO TURKEY MEATBALLS 120
    MOROCCAN CHICKEN 121

    ORANGE CHICKEN MEAL 123

    SAUCY CAJUN CHICKEN 124

    CREAM CHEESE CHICKEN 125

    TURKEY BREAST WITH HERBS 126

    WHITE CHICKEN WITH CAULIFLOWER 127

    ITALIAN CHICKEN THIGHS 128

    THAI BOWL 129

PORK, BEEF AND LAMB 131

    BUTTER LAMB SHOULDER 131

    SPICY PULLED PORK FOR SANDWICHES 132

    SUCCULENT LAMB 134

    MEXICAN BEEF WITH TOMATO AND CHILIES 135

    BRAISED LAMB STEW 136

    CHILE PORK STEW 137

    BEEF RATATOUILLE 138

    LAMB SHANKS WITH TOMATOES 139

    MOROCCAN LAMB 140

    ITALIAN SHORT RIBS 142

    HERBED SPARE RIBS 143

    SWEET RIBS 144

    ROSEMARY BEEF ROAST RECIPE 145

    BROWN RICE AND LAMB 146

    PERNIL PORK 147

    TACO SOUP WITH BEEF 148

    CHILI PULLED PORK 149

    CROCK POT PORK RIBS 150

    HEARTY BEEF STEW 151

GARLIC TERIYAKI BEEF 152
PORK POZOLE 153
SHORTCUT PORK POSOLE 154
SIMPLE TOMATO PORK CHOPS 155
STUFFED LAMB WITH ONIONS 157
WHISKEY BLUES STEAK 158
GROUND BEEF SHAWARMA 159
ASIAN BEEF SHORT RIBS 160
CILANTRO MEAT BOWL 161
AMAZING APPLE PORK CHOPS 163
JUST PEACHY PORK CHOPS 164

SNACKS AND APPETIZERS 165
CHICKEN PATE 165
CHICKEN WINGS 166
BROCCOLI CHEESE STICKS 167
BACON SKEWERS 168
UNIQUE PARTY FOOD 169
PORK LETTUCE FOLDS 170
BRAISED PULLED HAM 171
MEDITERRANEAN OLIVE SPREAD 172
SPAGHETTI FRITTERS 173
CAULIFLOWER HUMMUS 174
BEEF BITES 175
CHICKEN WINGS 176
SEMI-SWEET MEATBALLS 177
SPICY PECANS 178
GARLIC BRUSSELS SPROUTS 179

OREGANO CHEESE DIP	181
TRADITIONAL BRITISH SCOTCH EGGS	182
TOMATO AND AVOCADO SALSA	183
CHESTNUT DIP	184
CHILI SCROLLS	185
DESSERTS	**186**
COCONUT CAKE WITH CHOCOLATE TOPPING	186
SWEET POTATO AND CINNAMON PATTIES	188
SWEET APPLE BUTTER	189
ASIAN MEATBALLS	190
CARROT FRITTERS	192
CHILI SCROLLS	193
PUMPKIN PIE PANCAKES	194
MAPLE APRICOT PIE	195
TORTILLA PORK BITES	197
COCOA BARS	198
SIMPLE CAKE	199
COCOA BALLS	200
PECAN BROWNIES	201
MONKEY BREAD	202
VANILLA MINT CAKE	203
APPLE LEMON PIE	205
BREWED COFFEE PIE	207
CRUSTLESS BEEF PIZZA	208
RASPBERRY MUFFINS WITH TOPPING	209
INDIAN PUDDING	211

BREAKFASTS

ALMOND FRITTATA

Serving: 6

Ingredients:

- ½ cup tomatoes, cubed
- 1 cup almond milk
- ½ cup beef, chopped
- 2 spring onions, chopped
- 12 eggs, whisked
- A pinch of salt and black pepper
- A drizzle of olive oil

Directions:

- In a bowl, mix the all the ingredients except the oil and whisk well.
- Grease the slow cooker with the oil then pour the frittata mix in the bowl, spread, cover and cook on low for 3 hours.
- Divide between plates and serve for breakfast.

Nutrition:

- Calories - 295
- Fat - 22,4
- Carbs - 3,9
- Protein - 20,8

HONEY SWEET RAISIN BREAD

Serving: 6-8

Ingredients:

- 1 ⅓ cups lukewarm water
- 1 tablespoon honey
- 2 teaspoons fast rising dried yeast
- 4 cups bread flour
- 1 teaspoon salt
- ½ cup raisins, previously soaked and drained for softness

Directions:

- Mix together water, honey and yeast. Set aside for a couple of minutes or until mixture starts to bubble.
- Combine flour and salt in a bowl. Make a well in the center.
- Pour in half of the yeast mixture into the well. Stir with a fork until sticky in consistency.
- Add remaining yeast mixture to flour. Mix to form a dough.
- Knead the dough on a floured surface for about 5 minutes or until smooth.
- Add the raisin and distribute evenly into the dough.
- Lightly dust with flour and form dough into a ball.
- Line your slow cooker with some parchment paper.

- Place the dough in the middle of slow cooker. Fold the parchment away from the dough to prevent sticking while cooking.
- Cover the slow cooker and cook on HIGH for 1 to 2 ½ hours, checking every 30 minutes after the first hour. The bread is done when light tapping gives a hollow sound and crust is golden brown. You can also measure the internal temperature. It should reached 190 ºF on an instant read thermometer.
- Cool before slicing.

Nutrition:

- Calories - 71
- Fat - 1.1 g
- Carbs - 13.6 g
- Protein - 2.0 g

VEGAN PUMPKIN COFFEE CAKE OATMEAL

Serving: 8

Ingredients:

- 4 ½ cups water
- 1 ½ cups steel cut oats
- 1 ½ cups pumpkin puree
- 2 teaspoons cinnamon
- 1 teaspoon allspice
- 1 teaspoon vanilla
- ¾ cup brown sugar

Directions:

- Place all ingredients except the brown sugar in the Instant Pot.
- Give a good stir.
- Close the lid and seal off the vent.
- Press the Manual button and cook for 3 minutes.
- Do natural pressure release.
- Once cooked, do natural pressure release.
- Top with brown sugar.

Nutrition:

- Calories - 253
- Carbs - 35.9g
- Protein - 9.7g
- Fat - 12.3g

COCOA CHERRY BOWLS

Serving: 4

Ingredients:

- 3 cups almond milk
- 2 tablespoons ground flaxseeds
- 2 tablespoons cocoa powder
- 1/3 cup cherries, pitted
- 3 tablespoons coconut sugar
- ½ teaspoon vanilla extract

Directions:

- In your slow cooker, mix all the ingredients, cover and cook on high for 3 hours.
- Divide everything into bowls and serve for breakfast.

Nutrition:

- Calories - 461
- Fat - 44,4
- Carbs - 23
- Protein - 5,3

GRANOLA CRUMBLE

Serving: 4

Ingredients:

- 3 tablespoon maple syrup
- 2 tablespoon apple juice
- ¼ teaspoon salt
- 4 green apples
- 7 oz. granola
- ¼ teaspoon ground cardamom
- 1 tablespoon butter

Directions:

- Peel the green apples and cut them into halves.
- Remove the seeds from the apples and chop into the small pieces.

- Place the chopped green apples in the slow cooker and add salt, apple juice, maple syrup, ground cardamom, and butter. Add the granola and stir everything together well.
- Close the slow cooker lid and cook the Granola Crumble for 4.5 hours on LOW.
- When the crumble is done,

Nutrition:

- Calories - 427
- Fat - 18.7
- Carbs - 62.48
- Protein - 5

MUSHROOM AND SPINACH OMELET PIE

Serving: 12

Ingredients:

- 7 Eggs
- ¼ cup Butter
- 2 Garlic Cloves, minced
- 8 ounces Mushrooms, sliced
- ½ tsp Pepper
- 1 cup grated Cheddar Cheese
- ½ cup Heavy Cream
- 5 ounces Fresh Spinach, chopped
- 2 tsp Baking Powder
- 2/3 cup Coconut Flour

Directions:

- Melt the butter in your IP on SAUTE.
- Add mushrooms and cook for 5 minutes.
- Add garlic and cook for an additional minute.
- Whisk together the eggs and heavy cream.
- Stir in the flour and baking powder.
- Add the remaining ingredients, including the garlicky mushrooms, and stir to combine.
- Grease a baking dish and pour the mixture into it.
- Cover with a foil.
- Pout 1 ½ cups water into your IP and lower the rack.
- Insert the baking dish inside and cook for 25 minutes on MANUAL.
- Do a quick pressure release.
- Serve and enjoy!

Nutrition:

- Calories - 148
- Fat - 10.6g
- Carbs - 2.5g
- Protein - 6.2g

BABY SPINACH EGG CUPS

Serving: 4

Ingredients:

- 6 Eggs
- ½ cup shredded Mozzarella Cheese
- 1 cup chopped Baby Spinach

- 14/4 cup crumbled Feta Cheese
- 1 Tomato, chopped
- ½ tsp salt
- 1 tsp Pepper
- ¼ tsp Garlic Powder
- 1 ½ cups Water

Directions:

- Pour the water into your IP and lower the trivet.
- Beat the eggs along with the spices.
- Stir in the tomato and cheeses.
- Grease 4 ramekins and divide the spinach between them.
- Pour the egg mixture over.
- Arrange the ramekins inside the IP and close the lid.
- Cook on HIGH for 8 minutes.
- Serve and enjoy!

Nutrition:

- Calories - 114
- Fat - 7g
- Carbs - 2g
- Protein - 11g

BOILED EGGS WITH SPINACH

Serving: 2

Ingredients:

- 1 lb spinach, chopped
- 4 large eggs
- 1 tbsp olives
- 3 tbsp olive oil
- 1 tbsp butter
- Spices: 1 tbsp mustard seeds
- 1 tbsp raw almonds
- ½ tsp chili flakes
- ½ tsp sea salt

Directions:

- Rinse the spinach thoroughly under cold running water and drain in a large colander.
- Set aside.
- Plug in the instant pot and pour in three cups of water in the stainless steel insert. Add eggs and close the lid. Adjust the steam release handle and press the "MANUAL" button. Set the timer for 4 minutes and cook on high pressure.
- When done, press the "Cancel" button and perform a quick pressure release by
- moving the pressure valve to the "Venting" position. Carefully, open the lid and Clean and pat dry the insert with a kitchen towel and place in the pot. Grease with some olive oil and press the "Saute" button.

- Add spinach and cook for 2-3 minutes, stirring occasionally.
- Now, stir in one tablespoon of butter and season with salt and chili flakes.
- Mix well and cook for one minute.
- Turn off the pot and sprinkle with nuts.
- Gently peel and slice each egg in half, lengthwise. Optionally, serve with sliced avocado and drizzle with some more olive oil.

Nutrition:

- Calories - 414
- Fat - 36.8g
- Carbs - 4.1g
- Protein - 17.7g

COTTAGE CHEESE AND PINE NUT EGG PIE

Serving: 6

Ingredients:

- 6 Eggs, beaten
- 2 tbsp. chopped Pine Nuts
- 1 Tomato, diced
- ¼ cup Heavy Cream
- 2 tbsp. chopped Basil
- ¼ cup grated Parmesan Cheese
- 1 cup Cottage Cheese
- Pinch of Salt
- Pinch of Pepper
- 1 ½ cups Water

Directions:

- Pour the water into the Instant Pot and lower the trivet.
- Combine all of the ingredients in a large bowl.
- Grease a baking dish and pour the mixture inside.
- Place the dish inside the IP and close the lid.
- Cook for 30 minutes on MANUAL.
- Release the pressure quickly.
- Serve and enjoy!

Nutrition:

- Calories - 182
- Fat - 13g
- Carbs - 3g
- Protein - 13g

HAZELNUT AND CHOCOLATE BANANA BREAD

Serving: 6

Ingredients:

- 2 cups all-purpose flour
- 2 teaspoons baking powder
- ½ teaspoon baking soda
- Pinch of salt
- 1 egg, whisked
- 1 cup brown sugar
- 1 cup yogurt
- ½ cup butter or coconut oil
- 1-2 teaspoons vanilla extract

- 4 ripe bananas, mashed
- ⅓ cup milk
- ¼ cup chocolate chips (dark chocolate preferred
- ½ cup hazelnuts, chopped
- 2 cups water

Directions:

- Grease a 6-cup Bundt pan with cooking spray and line it with parchment paper.
- In a bowl, mix the flour with the baking soda, baking powder, and salt.
- In a separate bowl, whisk together egg, sugar, milk, yogurt, vanilla and oil. At the end, whisk in mashed bananas.
- Combine the contents of both bowls.
- Fold in the hazelnuts and dark chocolate chips.
- Pour this mixture into the Bundt pan.
- Pour 2 cups of water into the Crock-Pot Express and place the steaming rack on top.
- Place the Bundt pan on top of the rack.
- Cover the pan with a piece of foil.
- Secure the lid of the pot and seal the valve.
- Press MULTIGRAIN.
- Set the timer for 1 hour at high pressure.
- Remove from pan, let cool and serve.

Nutrition:

- Calories - 576
- Fat - 23.4 g
- Carbs - 83.2 g
- Protein - 10.5 g

CREAMY CHICKEN STRIPS

Serving: 7

Ingredients:

- 1 cup cream
- 2-pound chicken breast, skinned, boneless
- 1 teaspoon chili powder
- 3 tablespoons flour
- 1 teaspoon oregano
- 1 teaspoon ground white pepper
- 1 teaspoon sriracha
- 6 oz. asparagus
- 1 teaspoon sage

Directions:

- Cut the chicken breast into the strips.
- Combine the chili powder, flour, oregano, ground white pepper, and sage together in a shallow bowl. Mix the mixture up and sprinkle the chicken strips with the spices.
- After this, pour the cream in the slow cooker.
- Chop the asparagus roughly and put the vegetables in the slow cooker.
- Add the sriracha and stir. Place the chicken strips in the slow cooker.
- Do not mix the ingredients. Close the slow cooker lid and cook the dish for 8 hours on LOW.
- Let the prepared dish cool briefly and serve it with the creamy gravy.
- Enjoy!

Nutrition:

- Calories - 311
- Fat - 18.8
- Carbs - 5.71
- Protein - 29

TURKISH BREAKFAST EGGS

Serving: 2

Ingredients:

- 1 ½ teaspoons olive oil
- 1 onion, finely sliced
- ½ red pepper, sliced
- 1 cup mushrooms, sliced
- 4 cherry tomatoes, halved
- ½ slice sourdough bread, cubed
- 2 eggs
- 1 tablespoon skimmed milk
- 2 tablespoons chives, finely chopped
- 2 tablespoons plain low-fat Greek yogurt to serve

Directions:

- In a frying pan, heat up the oil and add the onion, pepper, and mushrooms. Saute until softened.
- Oil the bottom of the slow cooker and spread the vegetables over it.
- Add the cherry tomatoes and bread.
- In a medium mixing bowl, whisk the eggs with the chives and milk. Pour over the tomatoes.
- Close the lid and cook for 5-6 hours

- Serve with yogurt.

Nutrition:

- Calories - 165
- Fat - 8 g
- Carbs - 13 g
- Protein - 9 g

COCOA CHERRY BOWLS

Serving: 4

Ingredients:

- 3 cups almond milk
- 2 tablespoons ground flaxseeds
- 2 tablespoons cocoa powder
- 1/3 cup cherries, pitted
- 3 tablespoons coconut sugar
- ½ teaspoon vanilla extract

Directions:

- In your slow cooker, mix all the ingredients, cover and cook on high for 3 hours.
- Divide everything into bowls and serve for breakfast.

Nutrition:

- Calories - 461
- Fat - 44,4
- Carbs - 23
- Protein - 5,3

MUSHROOM AND CHORIZO MIX

Serving: 2

Ingredients:

- 1 avocado, peeled, pitted and cubed
- ½ cup vegetable stock
- 1 pound chorizo, chopped
- 1 red bell pepper, chopped
- 8 mushrooms, chopped
- 1 small red onion, chopped
- 3 garlic cloves, minced
- ½ cup parsley, chopped
- 10 ounces beef, chopped

Directions:

- Add all the ingredients to your slow cooker, except the avocado.
- Cover and cook on low for 6 hours.
- Divide everything between plates, sprinkle avocado cubes on top and serve.

Nutrition:

- Calories - 1563
- Fat - 116,3
- Carbs - 25,9
- Protein - 103,6

BROCCOLI AND EGGS BREAKFAST

Serving: 6

Ingredients:

- 1 broccoli head, florets separated and chopped
- 2 tablespoons avocado oil
- 15 ounces cooked turkey, sliced
- 12 eggs, whisked
- 6 spring onions, chopped
- 6 ounces coconut cream

Directions:

- Grease your slow cooker with the avocado oil then add all the ingredients, cover and cook on high heat for 5 hours.
- Divide between plates and serve for breakfast while warm.

Nutrition:

- Calories - 343
- Fat - 19,9
- Carbs - 7,6
- Protein - 34,5

SQUASH CINNAMON PORRIDGE

Serving: 2

Ingredients:

- ½ cup chicken broth
- 2 tablespoons maple syrup
- 2 tablespoons gelatin
- ½ teaspoon ground cinnamon
- ⅛ teaspoon ground ginger
- ⅛ teaspoon ground cloves
- 1 (1¼-pound whole squash
- 2 medium apples, cored and chopped roughly
- Pinch of salt

Directions:

- Switch on the pot after placing it on a clean and dry platform.
- Open the pot lid and place the squash, apples, broth, and spices in the cooking pot area. Give the ingredients a little stir.
- Close the pot by closing the top lid. Also, ensure to seal the valve.
- Press "MANUAL" cooking function and set cooking time to 8 minutes. It will start cooking after a few minutes. Let the pot mix cook under pressure until the timer reads zero.
- Press "Cancel" cooking function and press "Natural release (NPR)" setting. It will take 8-10 minutes for natural pressure release.

- Open the pot. Cool down the mixture and then Cut the squash in half lengthwise and discard the seeds.
- In a blender, add the squash, apple mixture from the pot, maple syrup, gelatin, and salt. Blend on a pulse mode until smooth.
- Serve warm. Enjoy it with your loved one!

Nutrition:

- Calories - 312
- Fat - 0.8g
- Carbs - 44g
- Protein - 13.5g

SPINACH FRITTATA

Serving: 2

Ingredients:

- 3 eggs, whisked
- 1 tablespoon crushed tomatoes
- 1 cup spinach, chopped
- 1/3 teaspoon salt
- 1 teaspoon ground paprika
- ½ teaspoon oregano
- 1 tablespoon sour cream

Directions:

- Place the chopped spinach in the blender and blend until smooth.

- In the mixing bowl, mix up together blended spinach, crushed tomatoes, eggs, salt, ground paprika, oregano, and sour cream.
- With the help of the spoon stir the mixture and Flatten it with the help of the spatula if needed.
- Close the lid and cook Fritatta for 3 hours on Low or until the mixture is set.

Nutrition:

- Calories - 118
- Fat - 8.1
- Carbs - 2.8
- Protein - 9.3

LOADED BREAKFAST POTATOES

Serving: 4

Ingredients:

- 4 russet potatoes, scrubbed
- 1-pound pork sausage, chopped
- ¼ cup onion, diced
- 1 red bell pepper, diced
- 1 orange bell pepper, diced
- ½ teaspoon garlic powder
- Salt and pepper to taste

Directions:

- Place the steamer rack in the Instant Pot and pour a cup of water.
- Place the potatoes on the rack.

- Close the lid and seal off the valve.
- Press the Manual button and adjust the cooking time to 20 minutes.
- Meanwhile, heat a skillet and place the pork sausage slices until the fat has slightly rendered.
- Add the rest of the vegetables and season with garlic powder, salt, and pepper to taste.
- Once the Instant Pot is done cooking the potatoes, take the potatoes out and place on a plate.
- Pour over the sausage and vegetable mixture.

Nutrition:

- Calories - 570
- Carbs - 73.8g
- Protein - 20.6g
- Fat - 22.4g

BREAKFAST SAUSAGE AND SPINACH FRITTATA

Serving: 8

Ingredients:

- 1-2 tablespoons coconut oil plus a little extra for greasing
- 1 ⅓ cups country-style sausage if this is not available then you can use any sausage of choice (the sausage should be chopped, fresh and free from soy, wheat, sugar or nitrites and all other additives
- 8 eggs, beaten

- 3/4 cups spinach (drained, if frozen)
- 1 large red bell pepper, seeded and diced
- 1 small red onion, sliced thinly
- Sea salt and freshly-ground black pepper, to taste

Directions:

- Line the inside of the slow cooker with parchment paper and grease with oil (This can be used as a handle later to easily pull out the finished product).
- Heat the oil in a skillet over a medium heat and saute the chopped sausage until
- slightly browned at edges (about 3-5 minutes). Remove from heat.
- Add all the ingredients to the slow cooker.
- Cook on LOW for 2 to 3 hours or until set.
- Let it cool slightly before cutting into individual.

Nutrition:

- Calories - 238
- Fat - 16g
- Carbs - 3 g
- Protein - 20 g

BREAKFAST LOAF

Serving: 8

Ingredients:

- ¼ cup butter
- 1 cup onion, diced

- 2 cloves garlic, crushed and minced
- 1 cup mushrooms, chopped
- 1 pound ground beef
- 1 pound ground pork
- 2 eggs
- ½ cup goat cheese
- 1 tablespoon sugar free maple syrup
- ½ cup almond flour
- 1 teaspoon ground sage
- 1 teaspoon thyme
- 1 teaspoon fennel seeds
- 1 teaspoon salt
- 1 teaspoon black pepper

Directions:

- Place the butter in a skillet over medium heat.
- Add the onion, garlic, and mushrooms. Saute for 3-4 minutes. Remove them from the heat and let them cool.
- In a large bowl, combine the ground beef, ground pork, eggs, goat cheese, maple syrup, almond flour, sage, thyme, fennel, salt, black pepper, and the cooled sauteed vegetables.
- Mix, using your hands, until all the ingredients are blended.
- Form the mixture into a loaf and place it in a slow cooker.
- Cover and cook on low for 8 hours.

Nutrition:

- Calories - 485.2
- Fat - 39 g
- Carbs - 3.5 g
- Protein - 29.3 g

VEGETABLES AND VEGAN

CARROTS AND TURNIPS

Serving: 2-4

Ingredients:

- 1 tbsp olive oil
- 1 small onion, chopped
- 3 medium carrots, sliced
- 2 medium turnips, peeled and sliced
- 1 tsp ground cu minutes
- 1 tsp lemon juice
- Salt and ground black pepper to the taste
- 1 cup water

Directions:

- Press the SAUTe button on the Instant Pot and heat the oil.
- Add the onion and saute for 2 minutes until fragrant.
- Add the carrots, turnips, cumin, and lemon juice.
- Saute for 1 minute more.

- Season with salt and pepper, stir well.
- Pour in the water. Close and lock the lid.
- Press the CANCEL key to stop the SAUTe function.
- Select MANUAL and cook at HIGH pressure for 7 minutes.
- Once timer goes off, use aQuick Release.
- Carefully unlock the lid.
- Taste for seasoning. Serve.

VEGETARIAN PASTA RECIPE

Serving: 6

Ingredients:

- Non-stick cooking spray
- 3 cans (14½ ounces each diced tomatoes with basil, oregano, and garlic
- 2 cans (14 ounces each) artichoke hearts, drained, quartered
- 1 tablespoon bottled garlic, minced
- ½ cup whipping cream
- 12 ounces dried linguine or pasta of your choice, cooked, drained
- Pimiento-stuffed green olives, sliced and/or pitted ripe olives, sliced
- (optional)
- Feta cheese, crumbled or Parmesan cheese, finely grated (optional)

Directions:

- Grease a crockpot and place two drained cans of diced tomatoes inside.
- Add in the remaining can of tomatoes (undrained), the artichoke hearts, and the minced garlic.
- Cook everything on LOW for 6 to 8 hours.
- Pour the cream into the mixture and stir. Leave for 5 minutes.
- Pour the mixture over the cooked pasta and top with optional ingredients.
- Serve and enjoy.

Nutrition:

- Calories - 403
- Fat - 8 g
- Carbs - 68 g
- Protein - 13 g

SLOW COOKED TOMATO CREAM

Serving: 4

Ingredients:

- 2 14 ounce cans crushed tomatoes
- 1 teaspoon mixed herbs (oregano, basil, thyme etc.
- 4 cups vegetable broth
- 1 cup heavy cream
- 2 tablespoons butter
- Salt and pepper

Directions:

- Place tomatoes, herbs, and broth in slow cooker and stir well.
- Cover and cook for 8 hours on LOW.
- Blend the soup, strain the solids out, and pour it back into the slow cooker.
- Add cream and butter and cook on LOW for 10 minutes. Season with salt and pepper to taste.

Nutrition:

- Calories - 160
- Fat - 5 g
- Carbs - 25 g
- Protein - 3 g

RICED ZUCCHINI WITH CHEESE

Serving: 4-6

Ingredients:

- 2 cups water
- 2 lbs Yukon gold potatoes, peeled and cubed
- ¾ lb parsnips, cut into
- 1 inch thick
- pieces
- 1 tsp sea salt
- 1 tsp ground black pepper
- 5 tbsp half and half
- 2 tbsp butter, melted

Directions:

- Prepare the Instant Pot by adding the water to the pot and placing the steamer basket in it.
- Put the potatoes and parsnips in the basket.
- Close and lock the lid. Select MANUAL and cook at HIGH pressure for 7 minutes.
- When the timer goes off, use aQuick Release.
- Carefully open the lid.
- Stir well.
- Using a potato masher or electric beater, slowly blend half and half and butter into vegetables until smooth and creamy.
- Serve warm.

LOADED POTATOES

Serving: 4

Ingredients:

- 4 large potatoes, halved, not peeled
- 1 cup black beans, cooked
- 1 cup sweet corn
- 1 cup vegan cheddar cheese
- 2 bell peppers, diced
- 2 tablespoons taco seasoning
- 2 tablespoons olive oil
- Optional toppings: "Beefless" ground beef
- Avocado
- Vegan sour cream

Directions:

- Toss potatoes in olive oil and cook on high for 3 hours, until slightly tender.
- Fill the center of the potatoes with cheese, beans, corn, peppers, and seasoning. Cook on high for another 2 hours until potatoes are fully cooked and the cheese is melted.
- Serve with desired toppings.

Nutrition:

- Calories - 442
- Fat - 17 g
- Carbs - 70 g
- Protein - 12 g

BUTTERNUT DAHL

Serving: 4

Ingredients:

- 1 cup red lentils, dry
- 2 cups butternut squash, peeled and cubed
- 2 cloves garlic, minced
- 2 tablespoons fresh ginger, peeled and minced
- 1 tablespoon curry powder
- 1 tablespoon soy sauce, low sodium
- 2 cups vegetable broth
- 1½ cups coconut milk, full fat

Directions:

- Add all ingredients to the slow cooker and cook covered on low for 8 hours.
- Serve warm over grain or with naan.

Nutrition:

- Calories - 385
- Fat - 19 g
- Carbs - 43 g
- Protein - 14 g

KETO VEGETABLE CREAM SOUP

Serving: 4

Ingredients:

- 1 cup heavy cream
- 2 cups cauliflower, chopped
- ¼ onion, diced
- 1 teaspoon olive oil
- 1 teaspoon salt
- 1 teaspoon ground paprika
- 1 oz celery stalk, chopped
- 1 cup chicken stock
- 1 tablespoon fresh dill, chopped
- ½ cup mushrooms

Directions:

- Put mushrooms, chicken stock, celery stalk, ground paprika, salt, and cauliflower in the crockpot.
- Add heavy cream and cook the mixture for 2.5 hours on High.
- Meanwhile, pour olive oil in the skillet.
- Add diced onion and cook it for 5 minutes. Stir it from time to time.
- When the time is over, open the crockpot lid and add diced onion and dill.
- Blend the soup with the help of the hand blender until creamy texture.
- After this, cook the soup for 30 minutes on High.

Nutrition:

- Calories - 138
- Fat - 12.6
- Carbs - 5.6
- Protein - 2.4

EASY SWEET POTATO RECIPE

Serving: 4-6

Ingredients:

- 2 cups water
- 6 medium sweet potatoes

Directions:

- Pour the water into the Instant Pot and set a steam rack in the pot.
- Wash the sweet potatoes and place on the steam rack.
- Close and lock the lid. Select MANUAL and cook at HIGH pressure for 12 minutes.
- When the timer goes off, use aQuick Release.
- Carefully open the lid.
- Serve or store in an airtight container in the refrigerator for up to 3 days.

ZUCCHINI LASAGNA

Serving: 2

Ingredients:

- 1 large egg, whisked
- 1/8 cup Parmesan cheese, grated
- 1 cup spinach, chopped
- 2 cups tomato sauce
- 2 zucchinis, 1/8-inch thick, pre-grilled

Directions:

- Mix egg with spinach and Parmesan.
- Spread the some of the tomato sauce on the bottom of the crockpot and season with salt and pepper.
- Spread the zucchini on a single the crockpot and pour over some of the tomato sauce. Repeat this for 2 to 3 layers.

- Top with Parmesan.

- Cover and cook for 4 hours.

Nutrition:

- Calories - 251
- Fat - 13.9 g
- Carbs - 4.8 g
- Protein - 20.8 g
- Serving suggestions: Garnish with fresh parsley.

MUSHROOM SOUP

Serving: 4

Ingredients:

- 1 cup cremini mushrooms, chopped
- ½ white onion, diced
- ¼ carrot, grated
- 1 garlic clove, diced
- 1 tablespoon fresh dill, chopped
- 1 teaspoon salt
- 1 teaspoon olive oil
- ¾ teaspoon ground black pepper
- 2 cups of water
- 1 cup of coconut milk

Directions:

- Put all ingredients in the crockpot and close the lid.
- Cook the soup for 7 hours on Low.

- When the soup is cooked, it is recommended to cool till the room temperature before serving.

Nutrition:

- Calories - 164
- Fat - 15.5
- Carbs - 6.7
- Protein - 2.3

POTATO AND HERBS

Serving: 4

Ingredients:

- 1 ½ pounds baby potatoes
- 3 tablespoons butter (melted
- 1 tablespoon dill
- Salt and pepper
- 1 teaspoon dried parsley for garnishing

Directions:

- Wash and dry the potatoes, and pierce on all sides.
- Place in the slow cooker, and add butter, dill, salt and pepper, and toss well.
- Cover and cook for 2-4 hours on HIGH, stirring occasionally.
- Once done garnish with parsley before serving.

Nutrition:

- Calories - 361

- Fat - 27.2 g
- Carbs - 27.8 g
- Protein - 3 g

INDIAN COCONUT KALE CURRY

Serving: 4

Ingredients:

- ¼ cup curry powder
- 1 can unsweetened coconut cream
- 1 package dry onion soup mix
- 2 cups kale, rinsed and shredded
- 1 large yellow bell pepper, cut into strips
- 1 cup cilantro for garnish

Directions:

- Place all ingredients in the Instant Pot.
- Stir the contents and close the lid.
- Close the lid and press the Manual button.
- Adjust the cooking time to 4 minutes.
- Do quick pressure release.
- Once the lid is open, garnish with cilantro.

Nutrition:

- Calories - 433
- Carbs - 15g
- Protein - 10g
- Fat - 42.7g

STUFFED BELL PEPPERS

Serving: 4

Ingredients:

- 4 red bell peppers
- ½ cup feta cheese
- 2 tbsp sharp cheddar, grated
- 2 tbsp gorgonzola, crumbled
- 2 tbsp almond flour
- ¼ cup fresh parsley, finely chopped
- 1 small onion, finely chopped
- 4 tbsp olive oil
- 3 tbsp butter, melted
- Spices: ¼ tsp salt
- 1 tsp dreid celery
- ¼ tsp dried rosemary
- ½ tsp black pepper, freshly ground

Directions:

- Rinse peppers and pat dry with a kitchen towel. Place on a cutting board and remove the steam of each pepper. Carefully remove the seeds and rinse well again. Set aside.
- In a small bowl, combine feta cheese, cheddar, gorgonzola, one tablespoon of olive oil, almond flour, parsley, and onions. Sprinkle with salt, celery, rosemary, and pepper. Mix well and set aside.
- Take a small baking dish and grease with the remaining oil. Tightly fit peppers in the baking dish and fill each with the cheese mixture.

- Cover with some aluminum foil and set aside.
- Plug in the instant pot and position a trivet at the bottom of the inner pot. Pour in one cup of water and place the baking pan.
- Seal the lid and set the steam release handle. Press the "MANUAL" button and set the timer for 15 minutes on high pressure.
- When done, perform a quick pressure release and open the lid.
- Optionally, top with some Greek yogurt before serving.

Nutrition:

- Calories - 329
- Fat - 30g
- Carbs - 9.8g
- Protein - 6.5g

BLACK BEAN SOUP

Serving: 2

Ingredients:

- 1 carrot, peeled and sliced
- ½ stalk celery, chopped
- ½ small onion, chopped
- 1 clove garlic, minced
- 1 cup black beans
- 3 cups chicken broth
- ½ cup stewed tomatoes
- 1 teaspoon Italian seasoning
- ¼ teaspoon cu minutes

- ½ teaspoon chili powder
- ¼ teaspoon cayenne pepper sauce
- ½ cup cooked brown rice

Directions:

- Combine all the ingredients in a 3-quart slow cooker, and stir.
- Cover, and cook for 4-6 hours on LOW. The vegetables should be fork tender.

Nutrition:

- Calories - 129
- Fat - 0 g
- Carbs - 24 g
- Protein - 8 g

CHEESY CORN

Serving: 4

Ingredients:

- 4 cups fresh or frozen corn
- ¾ cup cheddar cheese, shredded
- 8 ounces of cream cheese, cubed
- ¼ cup melted butter
- ½ cup heavy whipping cream
- ½ teaspoon salt
- ¼ teaspoon pepper

Directions:

- Combine all the ingredients in the cooker.

- Stir well and cover.
- Cook for 3-4 hours on LOW or until the cheese is melted.
- Stir well just before serving.

Nutrition:

- Calories - 218
- Fat - 10 g
- Carbs - 24 g
- Protein - 8 g

SUPER-FOOD CASSEROLE

Serving: 8

Ingredients:

- 6 organic eggs
- ½ cup heavy cream
- Salt and freshly ground black pepper, to taste
- 1 cup shredded cheddar cheese
- 2½ cups trimmed and chopped fresh kale
- 1 chopped small yellow onion
- 1 tsp Herbs de Provence

Directions:

- In a large bowl, add eggs, heavy cream, salt and black pepper and beat until well combined.
- Add remaining ingredients and mix well.
- Place the mixture into a baking dish evenly.
- In the bottom of Instant Pot, arrange a steamer trivet and pour 1 cup of water.

- Place the dish on top of the trivet.
- Secure the lid and place the pressure valve to "Seal" position.
- Select "MANUAL" and cook under "High Pressure" for about 20 minutes.
- Select the "Cancel" and carefully do a Natural release.
- Remove the lid and serve immediately.

Nutrition:

- Calories - 195
- Fat - 14.3g
- Carbs - 0.81g
- Protein - 11.4g

SPICY SWEET POTATO WEDGES

Serving: 4

Ingredients:

- 3 large sweet potatoes, peeled
- 1 cup water
- 2 tbsp vegetable oil
- ½ tsp kosher salt
- 1 tsp paprika
- 1 tbsp dry mango powder

Directions:

- Cut the potatoes into medium-sized wedges.
- Prepare the Instant Pot by adding the water to the pot and placing the steam rack in it.

- Place the sweet potatoes on the rack. Close and lock the lid.
- Select MANUAL and cook at HIGH pressure for 15 minutes.
- Once timer goes off, use aQuick Release.
- Carefully unlock the lid.
- Drain the liquid from the pot.
- Preheat the Instant Pot by selecting SAUTe. Add and heat the oil.
- Add the cooked sweet potatoes and saute the wedges for 3-5 minutes, until they turn brown.
- Season with salt, paprika, and mango powder.
- Stir well.
- Serve.

BROCCOLI CAULIFLOWER STIR FRY

Serving: 3

Ingredients:

- 2 cups cauliflower; chopped.
- 1 cup broccoli; chopped.
- 1 tablespoon olive oil
- 3 garlic cloves; finely chopped
- 2 eggs
- 1/4 teaspoon onion powder
- 1/4 teaspoon black pepper; ground.
- 1/4 teaspoon red pepper flakes
- 1/2 teaspoon salt

Directions:

- Plug in the instant pot and grease the stainless steel insert with olive oil. Press the "SAUTE" button and add garlic. Stir-fry for 2 minutes and add cauliflower and broccoli. Sprinkle with salt, pepper, red pepper flakes, and onion powder.
- Stir and cook for 5 minutes
- Now; add about 1/4 cup of water and cook for 5 more minutes, stirring occasionally.
- Poach the egg on top and season with some more salt. Cook for 2-3 minutes more and turn off the pot
- Using a large spatula, a
- serving plate. Optionally, top with sour cream or some Greek yogurt

Nutrition:

- Calories - 115
- Fat - 7.8g
- Carbs - 4.3g
- Protein - 6.1g

SIMPLE EGGPLANT SPREAD

Serving: 6

Ingredients:

- 4 tablespoon olive oil
- 2 pounds eggplant, sliced
- 4 garlic cloves
- 1 teaspoon salt

- 1 cup water
- 1 lemon, juiced
- 1 tablespoon tahini
- ¼ cup black olives, pitted and sliced
- A few sprigs of thyme
- A dash of extra virgin oil

Directions:

- Press the Saute button on the pressure cooker.
- Heat the oil and add the sliced eggplants. Fry the eggplants for 3 minutes on each side.
- Stir in the garlic and saute until fragrant. Season with salt.
- Add a cup of water and close the lid.
- Press the Manual button and adjust the cooking time to 6 minutes.
- Do natural pressure release and take the eggplants out and 7. Add salt, lemon juice, and tahini.
- Pulse until smooth.
- Place in a bowl and garnish with olives, thyme and a dash of extra virgin olive oil.

Nutrition:

- Calories - 155
- Carbs - 16.8g
- Protein - 2g
- Fat - 11.7g

SOUPS AND STEWS

CHANAFLOWER MASALA

Serving: 4

Ingredients:

- 2 cups chopped raw cauliflower
- 1 can chopped tomatoes
- 1 cup water
- 1 onion, minced
- 4 tbsp. chana masala mix
- 1 tbsp. oil
- salt and pepper

Directions:

- Warm the oil in your Instant Pot.
- Soften the onion 5 minutes.
- Mix all the ingredients in your Instant Pot.
- Seal and cook on Stew for 10 minutes.
- Release the pressure quickly and stir well.
- Rest before serving.

Nutrition:

- Calories - 100
- Fat - 5.5g
- Carbs - 10g
- Protein - 2g

TACO SOUP

Serving: 8

Ingredients:

- 1 lbs Ground Pork
- 1 lbs Ground Beef
- 16 oz Cream Cheese
- 20 oz Ro-Tel Diced Tomatoes and Green Chilies
- 2 tbsp. Taco Seasonings
- 4 cups Chicken Broth
- 2 tbsp. Coriander Leaves (chopped)
- ½ cup Monterey Jack (grated)

Directions:

- Set the Instant Pot to "Saute" and place in it the ground meats. Cook while frequently stirring and breaking larger chunks until all water has evaporated, some 10 minutes.
- Add the cream cheese, Ro-Tel and taco seasonings, and stir well to combine.
- Place and lock the lid and manually set cooking time to 15 minutes at high pressure.
- When done quick release the pressure. Stir in the coriander leaves.
- Serve topped with the grated Monterey Jack.

Nutrition:

- Calories - 547
- Fat - 43g
- Carbs - 4g

- Protein - 33g

ROSEMARY TURKEY AND KALE SOUP

Serving: 2

Ingredients:

- 2 carrots, sliced
- 2 cups turkey stock
- 1 sprig rosemary
- 2 cups turkey meat, bite-size pieces
- 2 cups kale, chopped

Directions:

- Saute onion, carrots and desired spices in a skillet, then add half of the stock to deglaze.
- Put the turkey in the crockpot and add the contents of the skillet.
- Cover and cook for 8 hours on low.
- Add the kale when cooked.

Nutrition:

- Calories - 403
- Fat - 28 g
- Carbs - 6 g
- Protein - 34 g
- Serving suggestions: Remove the turkey rosemary before serving.

- Tip: If the soup is to be served later, do not add the kale until just before serving.

ASIAN STYLE BROTH

Serving: 8

Ingredients:

- 1½ pounds assorted grass-fed chicken bones
- 1 pound assorted pork bones
- 1 chopped yellow onion
- 1 peeled and cut into three pieces medium carrot
- 8 cups filtered water
- 2 tbsp. fish sauce

Directions:

- In the pot of Instant Pot, add all ingredients.
- Secure the lid and place the pressure valve to "Seal" position.
- Select "MANUAL" and cook under "High Pressure" for about 120 minutes.
- Select the "Cancel" and carefully do a "Natural" release.
- Remove the lid and through a fine mesh strainer, strain the broth.
- Keep aside at room temperature to cool completely.
- Remove solidified fat from the top of the chilled broth.
- You can preserve this broth in the refrigerator for about 5-7 days or up to 3-4 months in the freezer.

Nutrition:

- Calories - 220
- Fat - 4.6g
- Carbs - 0.27g
- Protein - 39.9g

BEEF BORSCHT SOUP

Serving: 6

Ingredients:

- 2 pounds ground beef
- 3 beets, peeled and diced
- 3 stalks of celery, diced
- 2 large carrots, diced
- 2 cloves of garlic, diced
- 1 onion, diced
- 3 cups shredded cabbage
- 6 cups beef stock
- 1 bay leaf
- ½ tablespoon thyme
- Salt and pepper

Directions:

- Press the Saute button on the Instant Pot.
- Saute the beef for 5 minutes until slightly golden.
- Add all the rest of the ingredients in the Instant Pot.
- Close the lid and press the Manual button.
- Adjust the cooking time to 15 minutes.
- Do natural pressure release.

Nutrition:

- Calories - 477
- Carbs - 17.7g
- Protein - 44.5g
- Fat - 24.9g

EMERGENCY WHITE CHILI

Serving: 6

Ingredients:

- 1 ½lbs turkey, ground
- 20oz chicken stock
- 16oz chopped cauliflower
- 2 white onions
- 2 tbsp. Italian herbs
- 2 tbsp. paprika
- 2 tbsp. oil

Directions:

- Mix all the ingredients in your Instant Pot.
- Seal and cook on Stew for 30 minutes.
- Release the pressure naturally.

Nutrition:

- Calories - 265
- Fat - 16g
- Carbs - 4g
- Protein - 35g

CORN AND RED PEPPER CHOWDER

Serving: 4

Ingredients:

- 1 tablespoon olive oil
- ½ medium yellow onion, diced
- ½ medium red bell pepper, seeded and diced
- 2 medium red-skinned potatoes, diced
- 2 cups frozen sweet corn kernels, divided
- 2 cups vegetable broth
- ½ teaspoon ground cu minutes
- ¼ teaspoon smoked paprika
- Pinch cayenne pepper
- ½ teaspoon kosher salt
- ½ cup coconut milk
- Salt and black pepper to taste
- To garnish: chopped red bell pepper, corn kernels, and sliced scallions

Directions:

Nutrition:

- Calories - 85
- Fat - 2.2 g
- Carbs - 16.2 g
- Protein - 2.6 g

SUPER-QUICK CHILI

Serving: 6

Ingredients:

- 2 peeled and cubed carrots
- 1 chopped medium celery root
- 1 chopped small yellow onion
- 2 pounds cubed into ½-inch pieces grass-fed chicken breasts
- ¼ cup fresh lemon juice
- 1 tbsp. dried basil
- 1 tbsp. dried oregano
- 1 tbsp. dried cilantro
- 1 tbsp. ground cu minutes
- Salt, to taste
- 1 cup homemade chicken broth
- 1 cup chopped fresh cilantro

Directions:

- In the pot of Instant Pot, add all ingredients except fresh cilantro and stir to combine.
- Secure the lid and place the pressure valve to "Seal" position.
- Select "MANUAL" and cook under "High Pressure" for about 10 minutes.
- Select the "Cancel" and carefully do a "Natural" release.
- Remove the lid and stir in cilantro and serve.

Nutrition:

- Calories - 319
- Fat - 11.9g
- Carbs - 0.83g
- Protein - 45.4g

GINGER CARROT SOUP

Serving: 4

Ingredients:

- 6 carrots, peeled and chopped
- 1 sweet potato, peeled and chopped
- 1 onion, diced
- 4 cups vegetable broth
- 1 can coconut milk, unsweetened, full fat
- 1½ teaspoons curry powder
- 1 tablespoon fresh ginger, peeled and minced
- 1 clove garlic, minced

Directions:

- Combine all ingredients in the slow cooker. Cook on low for at least 7 hours, or on
- high for 3 hours.
- Use an immersion blender to blend the soup, or pour all ingredients into a traditional blender.
- Serve warm.

Nutrition:

- Calories - 220
- Fat - 12 g
- Carbs - 21 g
- Protein - 3 g

BEEF NECK STEW WITH PARMESAN

Serving: 6

Ingredients:

- For stew: 2 lbs beef neck, chopped into bite-sized pieces
- ½ eggplant, sliced
- 1 cup fire-roasted tomatoes
- 1 cup cauliflower, chopped into florets
- 3 cups beef broth
- 4 tbsp olive oil
- 4 tbsp Parmesan cheese
- Spices: ½ tsp salt
- ½ tsp chili powder
- 1 tbsp cayenne pepper
- 2 bay leaves

Directions:

- Rinse the meat and pat dry with a kitchen paper. Place on a large cutting board and cut into bite-sized pieces and place in a large bowl. Season with salt, cayenne pepper, and chili pepper. Set aside.

- Plug in the instant pot and press the "Saute" button. Grease the bottom of the inner pot with olive oil and add the meat.
- Cook for 5-7 minutes, stirring constantly.
- Now add the remaining ingredients and seal the lid. Adjust the steam release handle to the "Sealing" position and press the "Meat" button.
- Cook for 35 minutes on high pressure.
- When done, press the "Cancel" button to turn off the heat and release the pressure naturally. Make sure the pot stays covered for another 10 minutes before removing the lid.
- Carefully, remove the lid and chill for a while. Divide the stew between serving bowls and sprinkle each with Parmesan cheese.
- Serve immediately.

Nutrition:

- Calories - 414
- Fat - 20.6g
- Carbs - 2.8g
- Protein - 50.8g

CHICKEN VEAL STEW

Serving: 4

Ingredients:

- For stew: 1 lb veal cuts, chopped into bite-sized pieces
- 1 lb chicken boneless and skinless chicken breast, chopped into bite sized pieces

- 2 cups button mushrooms, sliced
- 1 cup cauliflower, chopped
- 1 cup cherry tomatoes, sliced
- 3 tbsp butter
- 2 tbsp olive oil
- 5 cups beef broth
- Spices: 1 tsp salt
- ½ black pepper, freshly ground
- 1 tbsp cayenne pepper
- 1 tsp smoked paprika
- 2 rosemary sprigs

Directions:

- Rinse well the meat and chop into bite-sized pieces. Generously sprinkle with salt and pepper.
- Place in two separate bowls and set aside.
- Plug in the instant pot and grease the inner pot with olive oil. Press the "Saute" button and add chopped veal. Cook for 4-5 minutes stirring constantly. Now add the chicken breast and continue to cook for another 3-4 minutes.
- Add mushrooms, cauliflower, and tomatoes. Sprinkle with cayenne pepper and
- smoked paprika.
- Continue to cook for 10 minutes.
- Finally, pour in the broth. Add rosemary sprigs and optionally season with some more salt and pepper to taste.
- Stir well and seal the lid.
- Set the steam release handle to the "Sealing" position and press the "MANUAL" button.
- Set the timer for 13 minutes on high pressure.

- When done, release the pressure naturally and carefully open the lid.
- Remove the rosemary sprigs and stir in the butter.
- Serve immediately.

Nutrition:

- Calories - 572
- Fat - 29.5g
- Carbs - 3.9g
- Protein - 68.6g

ITALIAN SAUSAGE KALE SOUP

Serving: 6

Ingredients:

- 1 lbs Hot Italian Sausage Stuffing
- 1 cup Onion (diced)
- 6 cloves Garlic (minced)
- 12 oz Cauliflower (frozen)
- 12 oz Kale (frozen)
- 3 cups Water
- ½ cup Heavy Cream
- ½ cup Parmesan Cheese (grated)

Directions:

- Set the Instant Pot to "Saute"
- Turn your pressure cooker on to Saute. Add in the Italian sausage stuffing and lightly brown,

- while constantly stirring to break the chunks, for 2 minutes.
- Add the onions and garlic, and mix well to combine.
- Add the cauliflower, kale and three cups of water.
- Place and lock the lid, and manually set cooking time to 3 minutes at high pressure.
- When done let naturally release the pressure and then quick release it.
- Slowly stir in the cream.
- Serve sprinkled with parmesan.

Nutrition:

- Calories - 400
- Fat - 33g
- Carbs - 7g
- Protein - 16g

WHOLE CHICKEN AND VEGETABLE STEW

Serving: 5

Ingredients:

- 1 whole chicken (3lbs)
- 10 oz. broccoli
- 7 oz. cauliflower
- 1 onion, finely chopped
- 1 tomato, chopped
- 3 tbsp. olive oil
- 4 cups chicken broth

- Spices: 2 tsp salt
- 1 tbsp. cayenne pepper
- ½ tsp black pepper

Directions:

- Clean the chicken and generously sprinkle with salt.
- Set aside.
- Plug in your instant pot and grease the bottom of the stainless steel insert with three tablespoons of olive oil. Press the "SAUTE" button and add finely chopped onions. Stir-fry for 3-4 minutes and add tomato.
- Continue to cook for another 5 minutes, stirring constantly.
- Now add the remaining ingredients and close the lid. Set the steam release handle and press the "MANUAL" button. Set the timer for 30 minutes and cook on high pressure.
- When done, press the "CANCEL" button and release the pressure naturally.
- Serve warm.

Nutrition:

- Calories - 554
- Fat - 18g
- Carbs - 6g
- Protein - 85.5g

ETHIOPIAN SPINACH AND LENTIL SOUP

Serving: 6

Ingredients:

- 2 tablespoons butter
- 1 tablespoon olive oil
- 1 onion, finely chopped
- 1 teaspoon garlic powder
- 2 teaspoons ground coriander
- ½ teaspoon cinnamon powder
- ½ teaspoon turmeric powder
- ¼ teaspoon clove powder
- ¼ teaspoon cayenne pepper
- ¼ teaspoon cardamom powder
- ¼ teaspoon nutmeg, grated
- 2 cups lentils, soaked overnight then rinsed
- 8 cups water
- Salt and pepper
- 2 cups spinach leaves, chopped
- 4 tablespoons lemon juice

Directions:

- Press the Saute button on the Instant Pot and heat the butter and olive oil.
- Saute the onion, garlic powder, coriander, cinnamon, turmeric, clove, cayenne pepper, cardamom, and nutmeg until fragrant.
- Add the lentils and season with salt and pepper to taste.
- Close the lid and press the Manual button.

- Adjust the cooking time to 60 minutes or until the beans are soft.
- Do quick pressure release.
- Once the lid is off, press the Saute button and add the spinach leaves and lemon juice. Simmer until the leaves have wilted.

Nutrition:

- Calories - 113
- Carbs - 11.9g
- Protein - 4.7g
- Fat - 6.7g

KOREAN ANCHOVY BROTH

Serving: 4

Ingredients:

- 1¼-ounce dried anchovies
- 4 cups filtered water

Directions:

- In the pot of Instant Pot, add all ingredients.
- Secure the lid and place the pressure valve to "Seal" position.
- Select "MANUAL" and cook under "High Pressure" for about 5 minutes.
- Select the "Cancel" and carefully do a "Natural" release for about 5 minutes and then do a "Quick" release.

- Remove the lid and through a fine mesh strainer, strain the broth.
- Keep aside at room temperature to cool completely.
- 5-7 days or up to 2-3 months in the freezer.

Nutrition:

- Calories - 19
- Fat - 0.9g
- Carbs - 0g
- Protein - 2.6g

LEMONY FISH BROTH

Serving: 9

Ingredients:

- 2 tbsp. olive oil
- 3 gills removed salmon heads
- 1 fishtail
- 1 chopped yellow onion
- 1 peeled and chopped carrot
- 1 chopped celery stalk
- 3 stalks parsley
- 1 fresh thyme sprig
- 2-3 lemon zest strips
- 4 tbsp. fresh lemon juice
- 1 bay leaf
- 1½ tsp coarse sea salt
- 9 cups filtered water

Directions:

- Place the oil in the Instant Pot and select "Saute". Then add the fish heads and tail and cook for about 2-3 minutes.
- Add remaining ingredients except for water and cook for about 2 minutes.
- Select the "Cancel" and stir in the water.
- Secure the lid and place the pressure valve to "Seal" position.
- Select "MANUAL" and cook under "High Pressure" for about 10 minutes.
- Select the "Cancel" and carefully do a "Natural" release.
- Remove the lid and through a fine mesh strainer, strain the broth.
- Keep aside at room temperature to cool completely.
- Remove solidified fat from the top of the chilled broth.
- You can preserve this broth in the refrigerator for about 5-7 days or up to 3-4 months in the freezer.

Nutrition:

- Calories - 104
- Fat - 6.3g
- Carbs - 0.23g
- Protein - 10.1g

POMODORO SOUP

Serving: 8

Ingredients:

- 3 tbsp vegan butter
- 1 onion, diced
- 3 lbs tomatoes, peeled and quartered
- 3½ cups vegetable broth
- 1 cup coconut cream

Directions:

- Preheat the Instant Pot by selecting SAUTe. Once hot, add the butter and melt it.
- Add the onion and saute for 5 minutes.
- Add the tomatoes and saute for another 2-3 minutes.
- Pour in the broth, stir. Close and lock the lid.
- Press the CANCEL button to reset the cooking program, then press the SOUP button and set the cooking time for 6 minutes.
- When the timer beeps, use aQuick Release.
- Carefully unlock the lid.
- Add the coconut cream and stir.
- Select SAUTe again and cook for 1-2 minutes.
- With an immersion blender, blend the soup to your desired texture.
- Serve.

HAM AND ASPARAGUS STEW

Serving: 6

Ingredients:

- 2.5 cups white asparagus, trimmed and chopped
- 2 cups chicken broth
- 1.5 cups diced lean ham
- 1 cup whole milk
- 2 tbsp. goat's cheese
- herbes de provence
- salt and pepper to taste

Directions:

- Mix everything in your Instant Pot.
- Seal and cook on Stew 25 minutes.
- Release the pressure naturally.
- If you like, blend into a soup.

Nutrition:

- Calories - 145
- Fat - 7.5g
- Carbs - 5g
- Protein - 15g

HOT AND SOUR SOUP

Serving: 6-8

Ingredients:

- 1 10-ounce package mushrooms, sliced
- 8 fresh shiitake mushroom caps, sliced
- 1 8-ounce can bamboo shoots, drained and julienned
- 4 cloves garlic, minced
- 1 15-ounce package tofu, cubed
- 2 tablespoons grated fresh ginger (divided
- 4 cups water
- 2 tablespoons vegan chicken-flavored bouillon
- 2 tablespoons soy sauce
- 1 teaspoon sesame oil
- 1 teaspoon chili paste
- 2 tablespoons rice wine vinegar
- 1 ½ cups peas, fresh or frozen

Directions:

- Combine mushrooms, bamboo shoots, garlic, tofu, 1 tablespoon of ginger, water, bouillon, soy sauce, sesame oil, chili paste, and vinegar in the slow cooker. Cook for 6-8 hours on LOW. The mushrooms and bamboo shoots should be tender.
- Add the peas and remaining 1 tablespoon ginger. Stir.
- Adjust taste with vinegar or chili paste, if needed.
- Serve with a few more drops sesame oil and the chili paste on the side.

Nutrition:

- Calories - 208
- Fat - 7 g
- Carbs - 22 g
- Protein - 19 g

INSTANT POT GOULASH

Serving: 5

Ingredients:

- 1 tablespoon olive oil
- 1 onion, chopped
- 3 cloves of garlic, minced
- 1-pound ground beef
- 2 carrots, chopped
- 3 cups beef broth
- 2 cans tomato sauce
- 2 cans diced tomatoes
- 1 tablespoon Worcestershire sauce
- ½ teaspoon dried thyme
- ½ teaspoon oregano
- 1 cup dry elbow pasta
- Salt and pepper to taste

Directions:

- Press the Saute button on the Instant Pot.
- Heat the oil and saute the onion and garlic until fragrant.
- Stir in the ground beef and stir for 3 minutes.
- Add the rest of the ingredients.

- Close the lid and press the Manual button.
- Adjust the cooking time to 15 minutes.
- Do quick pressure release.

Nutrition:

- Calories - 651
- Carbs - 81.5g
- Protein - 32.3g
- Fat - 18.9g

FISH AND SEAFOOD

TROUT WITH BROCCOLI

Serving: 5

Ingredients:

- 2 lbs. trout fillets, skin-on
- 2 tbsps. butter
- 2 tbsps. apple cider vinegar
- 4 cups fish stock
- 3 cups broccoli, chopped
- 1 small onion, finely chopped
- ¼ cup olive oil
- ½ tsp. chili flakes
- ¼ tsp. garlic powder
- ½ tsp. dried celery
- 1 tsp. chili powder
- ½ tsp. salt

Directions:

- Remove the fish from the refrigerator about an hour before using. Rub with olive oil and sprinkle with salt, dried celery, chili powder, chili flakes, and garlic powder. Place in a deep bowl and cover with a lid. Set aside.
- Plug in the Instant Pot and pour in the fish stock. Add broccoli and stir well. Seal the lid
- and set the steam release handle to the "Sealing" position. Set the timer for 20 minutes.
- When done, perform a quick pressure release and open the lid. Remove the cauliflower from the pot and drain. Place in a deep bowl and mash with a potato masher. Optionally, a
- food processor and process until smooth. Set aside.
- Place the steam insert in the pot and place the fish in it. Pour in 2 cups of water and seal the lid. Set the steam release handle again and press the "Fish" button.
- When done; perform a quick pressure release and open the lid. Remove the fish from the pot and press the "Saute" button.
- Add mashed broccoli and stir in the butter. Optionally, sprinkle with some salt and garlic powder. Heat up and remove from the pot. Serve with steamed fish.

Nutrition:

- Calories - 488
- Fat - 27.2g
- Protein - 54.2g

- Carbs - 3.3g
- Sugar - 0.0g

ADOBO SHRIMPS RECIPE

Serving: 4

Ingredients:

- 1-pound shrimps; peeled and deveined
- 2 tablespoon green onions; finely chopped
- 2 cups fish stock
- 1/4 cup soy sauce
- 1/4 cup olive oil
- 1/4 cup rice vinegar
- 1 small onion; finely chopped
- 1 red chili pepper; finely chopped.
- 5 garlic cloves; crushed
- 2 tablespoon fish sauce
- 1 tablespoon peppercorn
- 1 teaspoon stevia powder
- 2 teaspoon salt

Directions:

- In a large bowl, whisk together olive oil, rice vinegar, soy sauce, green onions, garlic, fish sauce, chopped onion, chili pepper, salt, peppercorn, and stevia
- Add shrimps and give it a good stir making sure to coat shrimps well in the marinade. a
- large Ziploc bag and refrigerate for at least 30 minutes (up to 2 hours)

- Plug in the instant pot and pour in the stock. Remove the shrimps from the Ziploc and place in the pot along with 1/4 cup of the marinade
- Stir well and seal the lid. Set the steam release handle to the "SEALING" position and press the "MANUAL" button
- Set the timer for 10 minutes. When done, perform a quick release and serve immediately.

Nutrition:

- Calories - 298
- Fat - 15.5g
- Carbs - 5.7g
- Protein - 30.4g

SIMPLE SALMON

Serving: 2

Ingredients:

- 2 salmon fillets
- 1 cup water
- Salt and ground black pepper to taste

Directions:

- Prepare the Instant Pot by adding the water to the pot and placing the steam rack in it.
- Season the salmon with salt and pepper.
- Place the salmon fillets on the steam rack and secure the lid.

- Press the STEAM button and set the cooking time for 10 minutes.
- When the timer beeps, use a
- Natural Release
- for 10 minutes.
- Uncover the pot.
- Serve with lemon wedges.

LEMON KALAMATA OLIVE SALMON

Serving: 3

Ingredients:

- 4 x 0.3 lb. salmon filets
- 2 tbsps. fresh lemon juice
- ¼ tsp. black pepper
- ½ cup red onion, sliced
- 1 tsp. herbs de Provence
- 1 can pitted kalamata olives
- 1tsp. sea salt
- ½ lemon, thinly sliced
- 1 cup fish broth
- ½ tsp. cu minutes
- ½ cup olive oil

Directions:

- Generously season salmon fillets with cumin, pepper, and salt; set your Instant Pot on "Saute" mode and heat the olive oil; add fish and brown both sides.

- Stir the remaining ingredients into the pot and bring to a simmer; lock lid. Set your pot on manual high for 10 minutes; when done, quick release pressure and then serve.

Nutrition:

- Calories - 440
- Fat - 34.0g
- Protein - 30.0g
- Carbs - 3.0g
- Carbs - 3.0g
- Sugar - 0.0g

CLASSIC SLOW COOKED TUNA NOODLE CASSEROLE

Serving: 6

Ingredients:

- 2 cups egg noodles
- Cooking spray
- 1 can condensed cream of mushroom soup
- ½ cup evaporated skim milk
- 2 5-ounce cans tuna in water, drained well
- ½ cup shredded cheddar cheese
- Salt and black pepper

Directions:

- Cook the noodles until just a little underdone (al dente. Drain.
- Coat slow cooker with non-stick cooking spray.

- In a large bowl, mix the soup and milk until well blended and creamy. Stir in the tuna and cheese. Stir in noodles and Cover and cook for 3 to 4 hours on LOW or for 1-1/2 to 2 hours on HIGH, stirring occasionally.

Nutrition:

- Calories - 300
- Fat - 5.3 g
- Carbs - 31.2 g
- Protein - 30.7g

SHRIMP CHOWDER

Serving: 3

Ingredients:

- 1 slice unsalted bacon, diced
- 6 oz shrimp
- 2 small red potatoes, scrubbed and diced
- 1/2 cup chopped onion
- 1 cup water
- 1/2 lb frozen corn
- 1/4 tsp black pepper
- 1/4 tsp paprika
- 6 oz fat free evaporated milk
- 2 Tbsp chives

Directions:

- Place a nonstick skillet over medium flame and cook the bacon until browned and slightly crisp. Stir in the onions and cook until tender.
- Drain as much fat as possible from the skillet, then Add the potatoes, shrimp, water, frozen corn, black pepper, and paprika into the slow cooker, then cover and cook for 3 hours on low.
- Add the milk and chives then cover and cook for an additional 20 minutes on low. Serve warm.

Nutrition:

- Calories - 257

MAHI MAHI CHILI

Serving: 4

Ingredients:

- 2 tablespoons butter, melted
- ¼ teaspoon salt
- 1/3 cup chopped green chilies
- 4 Mahi Mahi fillets
- ¼ teaspoon pepper
- 1 ½ cups water

Directions:

- Sprinkle the fish with pepper and salt.
- Take your Instant Pot; open the top lid. Plug it and turn it on.

- Press "SAUTe" setting and the pot will start heating up.
- In the cooking pot area, add the butter and fish. Cook for a minute per side.
- Pour the water and place steamer basket/trivet inside the pot; arrange the fish over the basket/trivet. Top with chilies.
- Close the top lid and seal its valve.
- Press "MANUAL" setting. Adjust cooking time to 5 minutes.
- Allow the recipe to cook for the set cooking time.
- After the set cooking time ends, press "CANCEL" and then press "QPR (Quick Pressure Release".
- Instant Pot will quickly release the pressure.
- Open the top lid, add the cooked recipe mix in serving plates.
- Serve and enjoy!

Nutrition:

- Calories - 315
- Fat - 22g
- Carbs - 5.5g
- Protein - 19.5g

ORANGE FISH

Serving: 7

Ingredients:

- 3 oranges, peeled, chopped
- 2-pound cod, peeled

- 1 tablespoon honey
- 1 garlic clove, peeled, sliced
- 1 teaspoon ground white pepper
- ½ teaspoon paprika
- 1 teaspoon chili flakes
- ½ teaspoon salt
- 2 tablespoons lemon juice
- 1 teaspoon olive oil
- ½ teaspoon honey

Directions:

- Sprinkle the cod with the ground white pepper, paprika, chili flakes, and salt. After this, sprinkle the fish with the lemon juice, olive oil, and 1 tablespoon honey.
- Combine the chopped oranges and sliced garlic together. Add the ½ teaspoon of honey. Stir carefully. Stuff the fish with the orange mix and wrap in the foil.
- Then place the wrapped fish in the slow cooker and close the lid. Cook the cod on HIGH for 3 hours. Then discard the foil and serve the cod. Enjoy!

Nutrition:

- Calories - 141
- Fat - 1.4
- Carbs - 11.74
- Protein - 21

CREOLE SHRIMP

Serving: 3

Ingredients:

- 3/4 cup sliced celery
- 1/3 cup chopped onion
- 4 oz unsalted tomato sauce
- 1/2 cup chopped green bell pepper
- 14 oz unsalted whole tomatoes
- 1/2 lb shrimp, peeled and deveined
- 1/4 tsp minced garlic
- 1/8 tsp pepper
- 3 drops hot pepper sauce

Directions:

- Place the onion, celery, tomato sauce, green bell pepper, garlic, pepper, and hot sauce into the slow cooker. Crush the whole tomatoes and mix in.
- Cover and cook for 2 hours on high or for 3 hours on low.
- Add the shrimp, cover and cook for an additional 1 hour on high. Best served over hot black or red rice.

Nutrition:

- Calories - 139

KETO SALMON MACARONI

Serving: 4

Ingredients:

- 8oz salmon steak; thinly sliced
- 1 cup fresh celery; finely chopped.
- 3 tablespoon butter
- 2 cups cauliflower; chopped
- 3 tablespoon almond flour
- 1 onion; finely chopped
- 1 cup heavy cream
- 1 cup cottage cheese
- 3 cups chicken stock
- 1/2 teaspoon black pepper; freshly ground.
- 2 teaspoon salt

Directions:

- Rinse well the steaks and pat-dry with a kitchen towel. Place on a large cutting board and cut into bite-sized pieces
- Plug in the instant pot and pour in the chicken stock. Add cauliflower and sprinkle with salt and pepper. Make a layer of thinly sliced salmon and seal the lid. Set the steam release handle to the "SEALING" position and press the "MANUAL" button. Set the timer for 5 minutes on high pressure
- When done, perform a quick release and open the pot. Remove the salmon and cauliflower and set aside

- Press the "SAUTE" button and grease the inner pot with butter. Add onions and cook for 2-3 minutes. Now add cottage cheese and heavy cream. Stir in celery and almond flour
- Briefly cook, for 3-4 minutes, stirring constantly. Remove from the pot and serve with salmon macaroni

Nutrition:

- Calories - 351
- Fat - 25.7g
- Carbs - 7.4g
- Protein - 21.8g

GINGER SQUID

Serving: 4

Ingredients:

- 1 cup Water
- 1 Rosemary Sprig
- 2 tbsp. Olive Oil
- 1 tsp Italian Seasoning
- ¼ tsp Pepper
- ¼ tsp Salt
- ¼ tsp Garlic Powder
- 1 cup halved Cherry Tomatoes
- 15 ounces Asparagus Spears

Directions:

- Pour the water into the Instant Pot.

- Season the salmon with salt, pepper, garlic powder, and Italian seasoning.
- Arrange on the rack.
- Add the rosemary sprig on top.
- Place the asparagus spears over.
- Top with cherry tomatoes.
- Close the lid and cook on HIGH for 3 minutes.
- Do a quick pressure release and Drizzle with olive oil.
- Serve and enjoy!

Nutrition:

- Calories - 470
- Fat - 31g
- Carbs - 4.6g
- Protein - 43g

SALMON PATTIES

- 1/3 cup coconut milk
- 1 tablespoon butter
- 1 tablespoon almond flour

Directions:

- In the mixing bowl, mix up together beaten egg, finely chopped salmon, dried dill, basil, salt, chili flakes, and almond flour.
- Toss the butter in the skillet and bring it to boil.
- Make the medium patties from the salmon mixture with the help of the spoon an put them in the melted butter.
- Roast patties 1 for 1 minute on the High heat.

- Close the lid and cook patties for 1 hour on High.

Nutrition:

- Calories - 271
- Fat - 21
- Carbs - 3.8
- Protein - 19.3

MEDITERRANEAN-STYLE COD

Serving: 6

Ingredients:

- 3 tablespoons butter
- 1 onion, sliced
- 1 ½ pounds fresh cod fillets
- Salt and pepper
- 1 lemon juice, freshly squeezed
- 1 can diced tomatoes

Directions:

- Press the Saute button on the Instant Pot.
- Heat the oil and saute the onion until fragrant.
- Stir in the rest of the ingredients.
- Give a good stir.
- Close the lid and press the Manual button.
- Adjust the cooking time to 10 minutes.
- Do natural pressure release.

Nutrition:

- Calories - 140
- Carbs - 2.5g
- Protein - 17.8g
- Fat - 6.4g

MISO TROUT

Serving: 5

Ingredients:

- 2-pounds trout
- 2 tablespoons miso paste
- 1 teaspoon fresh ginger, grated
- ¼ teaspoon nutmeg
- 1 tablespoon sesame seeds
- 4 cups fish stock
- 1 teaspoon salt
- 3 tablespoons chives

Directions:

- Pour the fish stock into the slow cooker. Add the miso paste and stir it with a wooden spoon until the miso paste is dissolved.
- After this, add the nutmeg, grated fresh ginger, sesame seeds, salt, and close the lid.
- Cook the liquid on LOW for 2 hours.
- Then, add the tuna and sprinkle it with the chives.

- Close the slow cooker lid and cook the dish for 20 minutes more. Serve the prepared miso trout with the cooking liquid. Enjoy!

Nutrition:

- Calories - 324
- Fat - 15
- Carbs - 2
- Protein - 43

SPICY AND SWEET TROUT

Serving: 2

Ingredients:

- 1-pound trout fillet; chopped
- 2 chili peppers; finely chopped.
- 3 tablespoon butter
- 2 tablespoon swerve
- 1/4 cup fish stock
- 1 tablespoon fish sauce
- 3 garlic cloves; crushed
- 1 tablespoon ginger; freshly grated
- 1/2 teaspoon cumin powder
- 1 teaspoon salt
- 1 teaspoon black pepper; freshly ground.

Directions:

- Generously rub fillets with salt and pepper. Place on a large plate and cover with aluminum foil, Set aside

- In a small bowl, whisk together fish stock, swerve, and fish sauce. Add grated ginger and cumin powder and stir well again
- Plug in the instant pot and set the steam basket. Place the fish fillets in the basket and generously brush with the previously prepared mixture on all sides
- Pour in one cup of water and seal the lid. Set the steam release handle to the "SEALING" position and press the "MANUAL" button. Set the timer for 5 minutes on high heat.
- When done; perform a quick release and carefully open the lid. Remove the fish and set aside
- Melt the butter over medium heat and drizzle over fish. Serve and enjoy

Nutrition:

- Calories - 600
- Fat - 36.8g
- Carbs - 2g
- Protein - 62g

TUNA STEAK WITH MUSHROOMS

Serving: 4

Ingredients:

- 2 large tuna steaks; about 8-ounce each
- 2 tablespoon olive oil
- 2 cups mushrooms
- 2 cups fish stock

- 1/4 cup Parmesan cheese
- 4 tablespoon butter
- 1 large onion; finely chopped.
- 1/2 cup heavy cream
- 1 teaspoon white pepper; freshly ground.
- 1 teaspoon dried marjoram
- 1 teaspoon sea salt

Directions:

- Plug in the instant pot and press the "SAUTE" button. Grease the inner pot with butter and heat up
- Add onions and stir-fry for 3-4 minutes, or until Pour in the stock and season with salt. Seal the lid and set the steam release handle to the "SEALING" position. Press the "MANUAL" button and set the timer for 5 minutes.
- When done; perform a quick pressure release and open the lid. Remove the steaks and place them to a bowl. Cover and set aside
- Now; press the "SAUTE" button and simmer the stock until the liquid has reduced in half. Add mushrooms and cook for 7-8 minutes, stirring occasionally.
- Season with salt, pepper, and marjoram and stir in the heavy cream and Parmesan cheese
- Give it a good stir and add tuna steaks. Drizzle with olive oil. Press the "CANCEL" button to turn off the pot and serve immediately.

Nutrition:

- Calories - 470
- Fat - 32.6g
- Carbs - 3.9g
- Protein - 39.1g

EASY CATFISH STEW

Serving: 2

Ingredients:

- 10 oz catfish fillets, cut into bite-sized pieces
- 2 cups fish stock
- 2 cups cherry tomatoes, chopped
- 2 cups collard greens, finely chopped (can be replaced with spinach or kale)
- 3 tbsp olive oil
- Spices: 1 tsp Italian seasoning
- ¼ tsp chili flakes
- 1 tsp garlic powder
- ½ tsp sea salt
- 1 tsp dried dill

Directions:

- Combine the ingredients in the instant pot and stir well. Seal the lid and set the
- steam release handle to the "Sealing" position.
- Press the "MANUAL" button and set the timer for 7 minutes on high pressure.

- When done, release the pressure for about 10 minutes and then move the pressure valve to the "Venting" position.
- Carefully open the lid and optionally sprinkle with some fresh parsley or grated Parmesan before serving.

Nutrition:

- Calories - 456
- Fat - 34.3g
- Carbs - 5.8g
- Protein - 29.9g

FISH WITH ORANGE AND GINGER SAUCE

Serving: 4

Ingredients:

- 4 white fish fillets
- Juice and zest of 1 lemon
- 1 thumb-size ginger, grated
- 1 tablespoon olive oil
- Salt and pepper
- 1 cup fish stock
- 4 spring onions, chopped

Directions:

- Place all ingredients except for the spring onions in the Instant Pot.
- Close the lid and press the Manual button.

- Adjust the cooking time to 6 minutes.
- Do natural pressure release.
- Once the lid is open, garnish the fish with spring onions.

Nutrition:

- Calories - 235
- Carbs - 3.1g
- Protein - 22.5 g
- Fat - 14.6g

CHICKEN AND POULTRY

TURKEY CASSEROLE

Serving: 6

Ingredients:

- 2 lbs boneless turkey breast, about 4 pieces
- 1 medium-sized onion, sliced
- 1 celery stalk, sliced
- 1 bag (10 oz frozen mixed vegetables
- ½ tsp salt
- ½ tsp ground black pepper
- 1 cup chicken broth
- 2 small cans of creamy mushroom soup
- 1 bag (14 oz) Pepperidge Farm herb stuffing mix

Directions:

- Add the onion, celery, and frozen mixed vegetables to the Instant Pot.

- Season the turkey breast with salt and pepper.
- Add the breasts to the pot. Pour the broth into the pot. Close and lock the lid.
- Select the POULTRY setting and set the cooking time for 25 minutes.
- When the timer goes off, use aQuick Release. Carefully open the lid.
- Pour the mushroom soup into the pot and add stuffing mix.
- Select the SAUTe setting and cook for another 8 minutes, stirring occasionally.

TURKEY MEATBALL STEW

Serving: 8

Ingredients:

- 2 14 ½-ounce cans Mexican-style stewed tomatoes, undrained
- 2 12-ounce packages frozen cooked Italian-style turkey meatballs, thawed
- 1 15-ounce can black beans, rinsed and drained
- 1 14-ounce can seasoned chicken broth with roasted garlic
- 1 10-ounce package frozen whole kernel corn, thawed (about 2 cups
- Salt and black pepper

Directions:

- Combine tomatoes, meatballs, drained beans, broth, and corn. Season with salt and pepper to taste.

- Cover and cook for 6 to 7 hours on LOW or for 3 to 3 ½ hours on HIGH.

Nutrition:

- Calories - 287
- Fat - 13 g
- Carbs - 30 g
- Protein - 16 g

DUCK LEGS IN BLACKBERRY SAUCE

Serving: 4

Ingredients:

- 4 duck legs
- 2 tablespoons blackberries
- 1 teaspoon liquid stevia
- ¼ teaspoon turmeric
- ½ teaspoon paprika
- 1 teaspoon salt
- 1/3 cup butter

Directions:

- Rub the duck legs with salt and Add butter and turmeric, and close the lid.
- Cook duck legs for 4 hours on High.
- Meanwhile, blend together blackberries, liquid stevia, and paprika.
- When the time of cooking is finished, open the lid and add blended blackberry mixture.

- Stir it carefully and close the lid.
- Cook the duck legs for 20 minutes on High.

Nutrition:

- Calories - 272
- Fat - 19.9
- Carbs - 0.7
- Protein - 22.1

CREAMY CHICKEN BACON CHOWDER

Serving: 6

Ingredients:

- 6 chicken thighs; boneless
- 8 -ounce cream cheese; full fat
- 4 tablespoon butter
- 1 teaspoon thyme
- 4 teaspoon minced garlic
- 1/2 cup celery
- 1/2 frozen onion; chopped
- 6 -ounce mushrooms; sliced.
- Salt; pepper, to taste
- 3 cups chicken broth
- 1 cup heavy cream
- 1-pound cooked bacon; chopped
- 2 cups fresh spinach

Directions:

- Cube chicken thighs and put inside Ziploc bag
- Add remaining ingredients to bag and seal. Refrigerate for 8 hours.
- Pour chicken mixture into Instant Pot, add chicken broth and cook for 30 minutes on "SOUP" setting
- Mix well, then stir in spinach and cream. Cover and let sit for 10 minutes to wilt the spinach. Top with chopped bacon. Serve hot.

Nutrition:

- Calories - 365
- Carbs - 7 g
- Carbs - 3.4 g
- Fat - 25 g
- Protein - 25g

TURKEY AND ORANGE SAUCE

Serving: 4

Ingredients:

- 4 turkey wings
- 2 tablespoons ghee, melted
- 2 tablespoons olive oil
- 1 and ½ cups cranberries, dried
- Salt and black pepper to the taste
- 1 yellow onion, roughly chopped
- 1 cup walnuts
- 1 cup orange juice

- 1 bunch thyme, chopped

Directions:

- In your slow cooker mix ghee with oil, turkey wings, cranberries, salt, pepper, onion, walnuts, orange juice and thyme, stir a bit, cover and cook on Low for 8 hours.
- Divide turkey and orange sauce between plates and serve.
- Enjoy!

Nutrition:

- Calories - 300
- Fat - 12
- Carbs - 17
- Protein - 1

ASIAN CHICKEN BOWL

Serving: 7

Ingredients:

- 3 oz orange juice
- 3 tablespoons sriracha
- 1 oz soy sauce
- 1 teaspoon olive oil
- 9 oz zucchini, chopped
- 1-pound chicken breast
- 9 oz cremini mushrooms
- 2 tablespoons fresh parsley
- 1 teaspoon salt

- 1 teaspoon ground ginger

Directions:

- Chop the chicken breast roughly and place it in the slow cooker bowl. Sprinkle the chicken breast with the salt, ground ginger, and olive oil.
- Combine the soy sauce, sriracha, and orange juice. Whisk it. Sprinkle the chicken breast with the soy sauce mixture.
- Slice the cremini mushrooms and chop the fresh parsley.
- Add the sliced mushrooms and fresh parsley to the slow cooker bowl.
- Close the lid and cook the dish on LOW for 8 hours.
- When the dish is cooked,

Nutrition:

- Calories - 247
- Fat - 7.8
- Carbs - 30.42
- Protein - 18

TURKEY AND MUSHROOMS IN A CREAMY WINE SAUCE

Serving: 10

Ingredients:

- 1 ¼ pounds Turkey Breast
- 1/3 cup White Wine

- 6 ounces White Button Mushrooms, sliced
- 1 tbsp. Arrowroot
- 1 Garlic Clove, minced
- 3 tbsp. minced Shallots
- 2 tbsp. Olive Oil
- ½ tsp Parsley
- 2/3 cup Chicken Stock
- 3 tbsp. Heavy Cream

Directions:

- Tie your Turkey every 2 inches, crosswise.
- Set your Instant Pot to SAUTE and heat the oil in it.
- Add the turkey and brown on all sides.
- Set aside.
- Add the shallots, mushrooms, garlic, and parsley, and cook for a few more minutes.
- Pour the broth over and return the turkey to the pot.
- Cook on HIGH for 15 minutes.
- Do a quick pressure release.
- Untie and slice it.
- Whisk the arrowroot and cram in the IP and cook until thickened.
- Drizzle the sauce over the turkey.
- Serve and enjoy!

Nutrition:

- Calories - 192
- Fat - 15g
- Carbs - 4.5g
- Protein - 25g

ROASTED CHICKEN WITH LEMON AND PARSLEY BUTTER

Serving: 2

Ingredients:

- 4 lb chicken, any part
- 1 whole lemon, sliced
- 2 tbsp butter or ghee
- 1 tbsp parsley, chopped

Directions:

- Rub chicken all over with salt and pepper to taste. Put it in the crockpot and pour 1 cup of water.
- Cover and cook for 3 hours on high.
- When cooked, add the lemon slices butter and parsley to the crockpot.
- Cook and cover for another 10 minutes.

Nutrition:

- Calories - 300
- Fat - 18 g
- Carbs - 1 g
- Protein - 29 g
- Serving suggestions: If you used whole chicken, chop to preferred parts before serving.

ONION CHICKEN

Serving: 5

Ingredients:

- 1-pound white onion, sliced
- 1 tablespoon butter
- 1 teaspoon sugar
- ¼ teaspoon salt
- 12 oz chicken wings
- 1 teaspoon ground black pepper
- 1 teaspoon turmeric
- 2 tablespoons balsamic vinegar
- 1 tablespoon soy sauce

Directions:

- Rub the chicken wings with the turmeric and ground black pepper.
- Sprinkle the chicken wings with the balsamic vinegar and soy sauce. Toss the butter in the slow cooker bowl and melt on HIGH for 10 minutes.
- Add the chicken wings in the slow cooker and close the lid. Cook the chicken wings for 4 hours on HIGH. After this, cover the chicken wings with the sliced onions.
- Sprinkle the onions with the sugar and salt and close the lid.
- Cook the dish on LOW for 4 hours. When all the components of the dish are soft, it is done.
- Serve the onion chicken hot. Enjoy!

Nutrition:

- Calories - 261
- Fat - 10.6
- Carbs - 23.92
- Protein - 17

MARINARA AND CHEESE STEWED CHICKEN

Serving: 6

Ingredients:

- 1 ½ pounds Chicken Meat (boneless thighs or breasts), cubed
- 15 ounces Chicken Broth
- 8 ounces Cheese (Monterey Jack or Cheddar), shredded
- 15 ounces Keto Marinara Sauce
- Salt and Pepper, to taste

Directions:

- Mix everything in your Instant Pot.
- Cover and lock the lid.
- Choose the MANUAL cooking mode and cook on HIGH for 15 minutes.
- Do a quick pressure release.
- Serve and enjoy!

Nutrition:

- Calories - 270
- Fat - 17g
- Carbs - 2g
- Protein - 21.5g

GREEN CHILI CHICKEN

Serving: 2

Ingredients:

- 2 chicken thighs, thawed
- 2 oz green chili
- 1 tsp garlic salt

Directions:

- Place chicken in the crockpot and cook for 6 hours on low.
- Drain the juices afterwards and add in the other two ingredients.
- Cover and cook for another 30 minutes on high.
- Shred chicken with a fork.

Nutrition:

- Calories - 347
- Fat - 23.8 g
- Carbs - 3.7 g
- Protein - 33.1 g
- Serving suggestions: Serve with tacos or wrapped in burrito.

TANGY CRANBERRY TURKEY

Serving: 4

Ingredients:

- 2 tablespoons olive oil
- 1½ cups cranberries, dried
- 1 yellow onion, roughly chopped
- 1 cup orange juice
- 1 cup walnuts
- 4 turkey wings
- 2 tablespoons ghee, melted
- A pinch of pepper and salt
- 1 bunch thyme, chopped

Directions:

- Switch on your instant pot after placing it on a clean and dry kitchen platform. Press "Saute" cooking function.
- Open the pot lid; add the oil, ghee, turkey, pepper, and salt in the pot; start cooking to
- brown evenly. Add the onion, walnuts, berries, and thyme to the pot; stir and cook for 2-3 minutes.
- Mix the orange juice, return turkey wings to pot, stir gently.
- Close the pot by closing the top lid. Also, ensure to seal the valve.
- Press "MANUAL" cooking function and set cooking time to 20 minutes. It will start cooking after a few minutes. Let the pot mix cook under pressure until the timer reads zero.

- Turn off and press "Cancel" cooking function. Quick release pressure.
- Open the pot. Divide turkey wings between plates and keep warm.
- Set instant pot on Simmer mode, cook cranberry mix for 4-5 minutes more. Drizzle the mix over turkey wings and serve warm!

Nutrition:

- Calories - 236
- Fat - 4g
- Carbs - 6g
- Protein - 15g

THAI CHICKEN SOUP

Serving: 6

Ingredients:

- 14 ounces canned coconut milk
- 1 butternut squash, peeled and cubed
- 1 yellow onion, chopped
- 2 cups veggie stock
- 1 tablespoon Thai chili sauce
- 1 and ½ tablespoons red curry paste
- 1 tablespoon ginger, grated
- A pinch of sea salt
- 1 pound chicken breast, skinless and boneless
- 2 garlic cloves, minced
- 2 red bell peppers, chopped
- Juice from 1 lime
- ½ cup cilantro, chopped

Directions:

- But the coconut milk in your slow cooker.
- Add squash pieces, onion, stock, Thai chili sauce, curry paste, ginger, a pinch of salt and garlic and stir really well.
- Add chicken breasts, toss to coat and cook on High for 4 hours.
- Add lime juice, stir soup, divide it into bowls, top with chopped parsley and bell peppers and serve right away.
- Enjoy!

Nutrition:

- Calories - 276
- Fat - 5
- Carbs - 8
- Protein - 16

FRAGRANT COCONUT CHICKEN

Serving: 6

Ingredients:

- 1 pound boneless chicken pieces, cubed
- ¼ cup butter, melted
- 1 tablespoon cu minutes
- 1 tablespoon ginger, freshly grated
- 2 teaspoons coriander
- 1 teaspoon cinnamon
- 1 teaspoon salt
- 1 teaspoon black pepper

- 1 cup onion, sliced
- 2 cups green beans, trimmed
- 2 cups broccoli florets
- 1 cup tomatoes, diced
- 4 cloves garlic, crushed and minced
- 1 tablespoon serrano pepper, diced
- 2 cups full fat coconut milk
- ½ cup unsweetened, shredded coconut
- ½ cup cashews, chopped

Directions:

- Place the chicken in the slow cooker and pour the melted butter over it.
- Season the chicken with the cumin, ginger, coriander, cinnamon, salt, and black pepper. Toss to coat.
- Add the onions, green beans, broccoli, tomatoes, garlic, and serrano peppers.
- Pour in the coconut milk and add the shredded coconut.
- Cover and cook on low for 8 hours.
- Serve garnished with chopped cashews.

Nutrition:

- Calories - 299.2
- Fat - 20.1 g
- Carbs - 11.3 g
- Protein - 21.1 g

POZOLE BLANCO

Serving: 4

Ingredients:

- 11 oz chicken breast, skinless, boneless, chopped
- 3 tablespoons almond butter
- 1 yellow onion, diced
- ½ teaspoon minced garlic
- ½ jalapeno pepper, chopped
- 1 teaspoon dried oregano
- 1 tablespoon lime juice
- ¾ teaspoon lime zest, grated
- ½ cup of water
- ¼ cup fresh cilantro, chopped

Directions:

- Put chopped chicken breast and 1 tablespoon of almond butter in the skillet.
- Roast the poultry for 5 minutes over the medium heat.
- Then onion, minced garlic, chopped jalapeno pepper, dried oregano, lime juice, and lime zest.
- Mix up the ingredients and pour water.
- Close the lid and cook the meal for 3.5 hours on High.
- When Pozole Blanco is cooked,

Nutrition:

- Calories - 176
- Fat - 8.8

- Carbs - 5.4
- Protein - 19.5

BUFFALO CHICKEN SALAD

Serving: 3

Ingredients:

- ¾ lb chicken breast halves, skinless, boneless
- 2 tsp apple cider vinegar
- ½ tsp paprika
- 1 Tbsp fat free milk
- 1 romaine heart, chopped into bite sized pieces
- ¼ cup thinly sliced red onion
- 4 Tbsp low sodium buffalo sauce
- ½ tsp Worcestershire sauce
- 3 Tbsp light mayonnaise
- 1 Tbsp blue cheese, crumbled
- ½ cup whole grain croutons

Directions:

- Place the chicken in the slow cooker. Add buffalo sauce, half the vinegar and Worcestershire sauce into a bowl and stir well.
- Spread the sauce mixture all over the chicken. Season with paprika.
- Cover and cook for 3-4 hours or for 1 ½ -2 hours on high.
- Remove chicken with a slotted spoon and place on your cutting board. When cool enough to handle, shred or chop into pieces.

- To make the dressing: Add mayonnaise, milk, and remaining vinegar into a bowl. Whisk well. Add blue cheese and stir well.
- Divide the romaine lettuce into 3 serving bowls. Divide the chicken and place over the lettuce. Spoon the dressing over the chicken.
- Scatter the onions and croutons on top and serve.

Nutrition:

- Calories - 274

MARINATED CHICKEN FILLETS

Serving: 4

Ingredients:

- 10-ounce chicken fillets; sliced into half-inch thick slices
- 2 garlic cloves; crushed
- 3 tablespoon apple cider vinegar
- 1 lemon; sliced
- 1 cup olive oil
- 1 tablespoon fresh oregano leaves
- 1 teaspoon dried thyme
- 1 tablespoon Dijon mustard
- 1/2 teaspoon dried rosemary
- 1 fresh rosemary sprig
- 1 teaspoon dried marjoram
- 1 teaspoon sea salt

Directions:

- In a small bowl, combine together olive oil, garlic cloves, mustard, apple cider, and spices. Add sliced lemon and mix well.
- Rinse the meat and pat dry with a kitchen paper. Submerge each piece into the
- marinade and When done, remove the meat from the refrigerator and let it sit for 10 minutes.
- Meanwhile, plug in the instant pot and set the trivet at the bottom of the stainless steel insert. Pour in 1 cup of water and place the steam basket on top
- Add fillets and drizzle with some of the marinade - about 3 tablespoons.
- Arrange the lemon slices on top and seal the lid
- Set the steam release handle to the "SEALING" position and press the "MANUAL" button. Set the timer for 13 minutes on high pressure.
- When done, perform a quick release and open the lid. Serve hot and enjoy!
- Optionally, brown the fillets for 2-3 minutes in a large non-stick pan over medium-high heat

Nutrition:

- Calories - 574
- Fat - 55.8g
- Carbs - 0.6g
- Protein - 20.8g

LIME AND SALSA CHICKEN WITH CAULIFLOWER RICE

Serving: 4

Ingredients:

- 2 Chicken Breasts
- ¼ cup Lime Juice
- ½ cup Mexican Cheese Blend
- ½ tsp Garlic Powder
- 3 tbsp. Olive Oil
- ½ cup Tomato Sauce
- ½ cup Salsa
- 2 cups riced Cauliflower
- Salt and Pepper, to taste

Directions:

- Combine all of the ingredients, except the cauliflower and cheese, in your IP.
- Close the lid and set the MANUAL cooking mode.
- Cook on HIGH for 12 minutes.
- Do a quick pressure release and add stir in the rice and cheese.
- Cook for 5 more minutes.
- Do a quick pressure release.
- Serve and enjoy!

Nutrition:

- Calories - 280
- Fat - 16g
- Carbs - 5g
- Protein - 19g

GROUND TURKEY SOUP

Serving: 6

Ingredients:

- 1 zucchini
- 1 carrot
- 1 red onion
- 1/3 cup white beans, cooked
- 1 tomato
- 1 teaspoon salt
- 1 teaspoon ground cu minutes
- 1 teaspoon cilantro
- ½ teaspoon paprika
- 10 oz ground turkey
- 1 tablespoon sour cream
- 1 teaspoon butter
- 2 garlic cloves
- 1 cup fresh dill
- 4 cups chicken stock

Directions:

- Put the ground turkey in the slow cooker. Add butter and sour cream.

- Mix and close the slow cooker lid. Cook the dish on HIGH for 2 hours. Meanwhile, peel the carrots, red onion, and garlic cloves. Chop the vegetables into the pieces.
- Combine the salt, ground cumin, and cilantro together.
- Chop the fresh dill and tomatoes. When the time is done, add the cooked white beans, spices, and chopped tomatoes in the slow cooker. a dd the chopped vegetables and paprika. Add the chicken stock and close the lid. Cook the soup for 3 hours on HIGH. When the soup is cooked, chill then ladle into bowls.
- Enjoy!

Nutrition:

- Calories - 193
- Fat - 6.7
- Carbs - 16.73
- Protein - 17

CURRY CHICKEN

Serving: 9

Ingredients:

- 22 oz chicken thighs
- 2 tablespoons curry
- 1 tablespoon curry paste
- 1 cup baby carrot
- 2 red onions
- 1 teaspoon fresh rosemary

- 1 teaspoon ground black pepper
- 1 teaspoon salt
- 3 tablespoons tomato juice
- 1 teaspoon butter
- 1 teaspoon minced garlic
- 2 cups beef stock
- 1 cup water

Directions:

- Put the chicken thighs in the slow cooker bowl.
- Combine the curry and curry paste together in the bowl. Add water and whisk it until the curry paste is dissolved. Wash the baby carrot carefully and toss them in the slow cooker bowl.
- Add fresh rosemary, ground black pepper, salt, tomato juice, and minced garlic.
- Then pour the curry mixture and beef stock in the bowl as well.
- Add butter and close the lid. Cook the curry chicken on LOW for 9 hours.
- When the chicken is cooked, discard ½ of the prepared liquid. Serve the curry chicken immediately.
- Enjoy!

Nutrition:

- Calories - 130
- Fat - 6.4
- Carbs - 4.98
- Protein - 14

COQ AU VIN

Serving: 8

Ingredients:

- 2 leeks, halved
- 2 sprigs fresh parsley
- 1 teaspoon bay leaf
- 2 tablespoons olive oil
- 3 pounds chicken thighs
- Fat - removed
- ¼ cup butter
- 8 ounces bacon, chopped
- 5 ounces button mushrooms, chopped
- 6 shallots, sliced
- 4 cloves garlic, crushed
- ⅓ cup flour
- ½ cup tomato paste
- 2 carrots, peeled, diced
- 2½ cups red wine
- 1 cup chicken stock
- Salt and black ground pepper, to taste

Directions:

- Press the BROWN/SAUTe button of the Crock-Pot Express and add oil.
- Preheat for 2 minutes, then press the START/STOP button.
- Add the chicken to the pot and cook it until brown.
- Add butter and bacon to the pot and cook it until crispy.

- Add the mushrooms, leeks, garlic and all the remaining ingredients except the flour and tomato paste.
- Cook for 8 minutes, until tender.
- Stir in flour and tomato paste.
- Secure the lid of the Crock-Pot Express.
- Press the POULTRY button and set the timer to 10 minutes at high pressure. The steam release valve should be closed.
- Serve hot.

Nutrition:

- Calories - 684
- Fat - 34 g
- Carbs - 16 g
- Protein - 62.5 g

JALAPENO TURKEY MEATBALLS

Serving: 6

Ingredients:

- 1 1/2 lb ground skinless turkey breasts
- 1/2 cup minced onion, divided
- 2 small egg whites
- 2/3 medium fresh jalapeno, seeded, minced
- 1/3 cup whole wheat bread crumbs
- 1 1/2 tsp chili powder, divided
- 2/3 tsp ground cumin, divided
- 2 medium garlic cloves, minced, divided
- 1/4 tsp sea salt, divided
- 3 tsp olive oil

- 18 oz canned unsalted diced tomatoes, undrained
- 12 oz unsalted tomato sauce
- 1/3 cup chopped fresh cilantro

Directions:

- In a bowl, mix together the ground turkey, bread crumbs, egg white, jalapeno, half each of the chili powder, cumin, garlic, onion, and salt using your hands. Form into 18 meatballs.
- Heat the oil over medium high flame in a nonstick skillet. Brown the meatballs, then set aside.
- In the slow cooker, combine the tomato sauce, tomatoes with their juices, remaining chili powder, onion cumin, garlic clove, and salt. Add the meatballs, turning to coat.
- Cover and cook for 10 hours on low or for 5 hours on high.
- Stir in the cilantro, then serve.

Nutrition:

- Calories - 237

MOROCCAN CHICKEN

Serving: 6

Ingredients:

- 1/2 cup chicken broth
- 2 garlic cloves, minced
- 1 yellow onion, sliced thinly

- Juice and zest of 1/2 navel orange
- 1/4 cup dry white wine
- 1/2 tsp ground ginger
- 1/2 tsp ground cu minutes
- 1/2 tsp ground coriander
- 1/4 tsp sea salt
- 1/4 tsp freshly cracked black pepper
- 1 cinnamon stick
- 1 1/2 lb skinless chicken breast or thighs, bone in
- 1/2 cup chopped pitted prunes
- Optional: 2 Tbsp toasted sliced almonds

Directions:

- Combine the wine, broth, orange zest and juice, coriander, cumin, ginger, garlic, salt, and pepper in a bowl. Mix well, then set aside.
- Arrange the chicken pieces in the slow cooker, then add the cinnamon stick on top,
- followed by the prunes and onion slices.
- Pour the wine mixture evenly into the slow cooker.
- Cover and cook for 2 hours and 30 minutes on high or for 4 hours on low, or until the chicken is completely done.
- Take out the cinnamon sticks, then sprinkle the toasted sliced almonds on top. Serve warm.

Nutrition:

- Calories - 234

ORANGE CHICKEN MEAL

Serving: 2-3

Ingredients:

- 2 tablespoons brown sugar
- 1/4 cup chicken stock
- 1 pound chicken breast, skinless and boneless, cut into small pieces
- Juice 1 orange or more to taste
- 1 tablespoon tomato ketchup
- 2 tablespoons flour
- 1 tablespoon coconut oil

Directions:

- Coat the chicken with the flour in a bowl.
- Set aside.
- Take your Instant Pot and open the top lid.
- Press "SAUTE" mode.
- Add the oil and heat it; stir-cook the chicken until evenly brown for 2-3 minutes.
- Add remaining ingredients; gently stir.
- Close the top lid and seal the pressure valve.
- Press "MANUAL" setting with 15 minutes of cooking time and "HIGH" pressure mode.
- Press "QPR" function to release the pressure.
- Open the lid; Enjoy!

Nutrition:

- Calories - 394
- Fat - 12g

- Carbs - 24g
- Sodium - 324mg
- Protein - 46g

SAUCY CAJUN CHICKEN

Serving: 6

Ingredients:

- 8 chicken drumsticks, 5 oz each, skin and visible fat removed
- 8 oz unsalted tomato sauce
- 2 tsp Worcestershire sauce
- 1 Tbsp milk Louisiana style hot pepper sauce
- 1 tsp crumbled dried thyme
- 1/4 tsp sea salt
- 1 1/2 tsp crumbled dried oregano
- 1/2 tsp garlic powder
- 10 oz frozen brown rice

Directions:

- Coat the slow cooker with nonstick cooking spray. Place the chicken drumsticks inside.
- Combine the tomato sauce, Worcestershire sauce, pepper sauce, dried thyme, sea salt, oregano, and garlic powder in a bowl, then pour all over the chicken. Turn chicken to coat.
- Cover and cook for 3 hours on high or for 6 hours on low, or until chicken is cooked through.
- Cook rice based on manufacturer's instructions, then place on a platter.

- Arrange the chicken on top of the rice and drizzle the sauce all over. Serve warm.

Nutrition:

- Calories - 205

CREAM CHEESE CHICKEN

Serving: 6

Ingredients:

- 1 lb chicken breasts, boneless and skinless
- 1 can (10 oz rotel tomato, undrained
- 1 can (15 oz) corn, undrained
- 1 can (15 oz) black beans, drained and rinsed
- 1 package (1 oz) dry ranch seasoning
- 1½ tsp chili powder
- 1½ tsp cu minutes
- 8 oz cream cheese
- ¼ cup parsley

Directions:

- Combine all of the ingredients, except cheese, in the Instant Pot.
- Close and lock the lid. Select MANUAL and cook at HIGH pressure for 20 minutes.
- When the timer goes off, let the pressure
- Release Naturally for 10 minutes, then release any remaining steam manually. Open the lid.
- Add the cheese to the pot and stir well. Close the lid a let sit for 5 minutes, until cheese is melted.

- Open the lid and return the chicken to the pot. Stir to combine.
- Top with parsley and serve.
- Notes: Serve with tortilla chips or rice.

TURKEY BREAST WITH HERBS

Serving: 2-4

Ingredients:

- 1 3- to 5-pound turkey breast
- sea salt and pepper, to taste
- 2 tablespoons gluten-free apple cider vinegar or lemon juice
- 6-8 fresh herb leaves such as sage, thyme, rosemary and/or parsley
- 2 tablespoons unsalted grass-fed butter (substitutes: ghee or coconut oil
- 4 cloves garlic, minced
- ½ cup water or homemade chicken broth

Directions:

- Season the turkey breast generously with salt and pepper.
- Make a paste with the vinegar, herbs, butter, and garlic.
- Carefully lift the skin off the turkey to make a pocket. Fill this with the herb paste. Spread any excess paste over the surface.
- Pour in the broth.
- Place the turkey breast, skin up, in the slow cooker. Be careful not to wash off the seasoning.

- Sprinkle with more black pepper and top with extra herbs, if desired.
- Cover and cook for 4 ½ to 6 hours on LOW or until the internal temperature reaches 165° F.
- Tent with aluminum foil and let rest for about 10 minutes before slicing.
- OPTIONAL:

Nutrition:

- Calories - 291
- Fat - 10.7 g
- Carbs - 2 g
- Protein - 44.3 g

WHITE CHICKEN WITH CAULIFLOWER

Serving: 4

Ingredients:

- 1 Butter Stick
- 4 Chicken Breasts, cubed
- 2 cups Cauliflower Florets
- 2 cups Heavy Cream
- 8 ounces Cream Cheese
- 1 tsp minced Garlic
- 1 tbsp. chopped Basil

Directions:

- Preheat your Instant Pot on SAUTE.
- Melt the butter inside.

- Whisk together the cream cheese and heavy cream inside.
- Stir in the remaining ingredients and close the lid.
- Cook on HIGH for 15 minutes.
- Do a quick pressure release.
- Serve and enjoy!

Nutrition:

- Calories - 700
- Fat - 40g
- Carbs - 5g
- Protein - 70g

ITALIAN CHICKEN THIGHS

Serving: 6

Ingredients:

- 6 Chicken Thighs
- 2 cups Cherry Tomatoes
- ½ cup Basil
- 3 Garlic Cloves, minced
- 1 Onion, chopped
- ½ pound Cremini Mushrooms, sliced
- ½ cup Olives
- 1 tbsp. Tomato Paste
- 1 tbsp. Olive Oil
- ¼ cup Parsley
- 1 cup Chicken Broth

Directions:

- Heat the olive oil in your IP on SAUTE.
- Sear the chicken until golden.
- Set aside.
- Add mushrooms and onions and cook for a few minutes.
- Add garlic and cook for 30 seconds.
- Stir in the remaining ingredients including the chicken, and close the lid.
- Cook on HIGH for 10 minutes.
- Do a quick pressure release.
- Serve and enjoy!

Nutrition:

- Calories - 245
- Fat - 25g
- Carbs - 7g
- Protein - 35g

THAI BOWL

Serving: 7

Ingredients:

- 9 oz turkey fillet
- 5 oz coconut milk
- 1 teaspoon salt
- 1 teaspoon turmeric
- 2 tablespoons peanut butter
- 6 oz noodles, cooked
- 6 oz red cabbage, sliced

- 1 jalapeno pepper
- 1 tablespoon oregano
- 1 tablespoon tomato paste
- 1 teaspoon fresh parsley, chopped

Directions:

- Chop the turkey fillet roughly and put it in the slow cooker bowl. Combine the coconut milk with salt, turmeric, peanut butter, oregano, tomato paste, and fresh parsley.
- Mix well. After this, sprinkle the turkey fillet with the coconut milk mixture. Slice the jalapeno pepper and add the sliced jalapeno into the slow cooker and close the lid.
- Cook the turkey for 4 hours on HIGH. Then add the cooked noodles and stir carefully with a spatula.
- Cook the dish on HIGH for 15 minutes more.
- Then Enjoy!

Nutrition:

- Calories - 279
- Fat - 22
- Carbs - 11.6
- Protein - 9

PORK, BEEF AND LAMB

BUTTER LAMB SHOULDER

Serving: 5

Ingredients:

- 2 lbs lamb shoulder, chopped
- 3 tbsp butter
- 2 cups beef broth
- ½ eggplant, cubed
- 4 garlic cloves, crushed
- 1 tomato, chopped
- Spices: 1 ½ tsp salt
- 1 tsp black pepper, ground
- 2 tsp cumin powder
- 2 tsp coriander powder
- 1 tsp onion powder
- 1 tbsp ginger, freshly grated
- 1 cinnamon stick

Directions:

- In a small bowl, combine salt, black pepper, cumin powder, coriander powder, and grated ginger.
- Set aside.
- Rinse well the meat and rub with spices.
- Set aside.
- Plug in the instant pot and press the "Saute" button. Grease the inner pot with butter and heat

up. Add meat, in several batches, and cook for 4-5 minutes, turning once.
- Remove from the pot and set aside.
- Now add eggplant and garlic. Season with some salt and cook for 5 minutes, stirring constantly. Add tomatoes and give it a good stir. Continue to cook for another minute.
- Now add the meat and pour in the broth.
- Seal the lid.
- Set the steam release handle to the "Sealing" position and press the "MANUAL" button.
- Cook for 25 minutes on high pressure.
- When done, release the pressure naturally and open the lid.
- Serve immediately.
- Optionally, use the "Slow Cooker" mode and cook for 8 hours on low.

Nutrition:

- Calories - 431
- Fat - 20.9g
- Carbs - 2.5g
- Protein - 53.7g

SPICY PULLED PORK FOR SANDWICHES

Serving: 7

Ingredients:

- 1 white onion, peeled and sliced
- 2 oz garlic, peeled and chopped

- 7 oz beef broth
- 1 tablespoon brown sugar
- ½ chili pepper, chopped
- ¼ tablespoon kosher salt
- 1 teaspoon ground coriander
- ¼ teaspoon ground ginger
- 1 tablespoon chili sauce
- 1 teaspoon cayenne pepper
- 1 teaspoon oregano
- 3-pounds pork shoulder
- 1 tablespoon dried dill

Directions:

- Combine the brown sugar and beef broth. Stir it until the sugar is dissolved. Combine the kosher salt, ground coriander, ground ginger, cayenne pepper, oregano, and dried dill.
- Chop the pork shoulder then toss the pork shoulder with the spices and stir. Add the chili sauce. Then Add the sweet beef broth mixture, sliced onion and garlic.
- Close the lid and cook the pork shoulder on LOW for 9 hours. When the meat is cooked, shred it carefully. Serve the spicy pulled pork with the sandwich bread. Enjoy!

Nutrition:

- Calories - 565
- Fat - 34.7
- Carbs - 10.26
- Protein - 50

SUCCULENT LAMB

Serving: 2

Ingredients:

- 2/3 lb. leg of lamb
- 2 tbsp whole -rain mustard
- 1/3 tbsp maple syrup
- 1 sprig thyme
- 1/4 tsp dried rosemary

Directions:

- Cut 3 slits across top of lamb. Put some garlic and rosemary in each slit.
- Add lamb to crock-pot and rub with olive oil, mustard, maple syrup, salt and pepper.
- Cook for 7 hours on low, add sprig of thyme, then cook for additional 1 hour.

Nutrition:

- Calories - 414
- Fat - 35.2g
- Carbs - 0.3g
- Protein - 26.7g,
- Serving suggestions: Add leaves of mint for extra flavor.

MEXICAN BEEF WITH TOMATO AND CHILIES

Serving: 2

Ingredients:

- 1 pound beef steak, round or sirloin
- 1 (10 ounce can diced tomatoes, with juices
- 1 tablespoon jalapeño, seeded and minced
- ½ medium onion, chopped
- 2 cloves garlic, minced
- ½ teaspoon ground cu minutes
- Salt and pepper to taste
- 1 (15 ounce) can pinto or navy beans
- 1 ½ cups hot cooked rice
- Garnishes: 3 tablespoons cheddar cheese, grated (optional)
- 2 tablespoons sour cream (optional)
- 2 tablespoons ripe olives, sliced
- 2 tablespoons green onion, sliced
- 2 tablespoons guacamole
- 2 tablespoons cilantro, chopped

Directions:

- Place the beef steak in a 2-quart slow cooker.
- In a medium-sized mixing bowl, combine the tomatoes, jalapeño, onion, garlic, cumin, salt, and pepper. Pour the mixture over the beef.
- Cover, and cook for 8 hours on LOW. The meat should be fork tender.

- When the cooking is done, remove the beef from the cooker and add the beans to the pan juices. Heat for 30 minutes.
- Meanwhile, slice the steak and arrange it over cooked rice. Spoon the bean mixture over everything, and top with your choice of garnishes!

Nutrition:

- Calories - 460
- Fat - 11 g
- Carbs - 52 g
- Protein - 38 g

BRAISED LAMB STEW

Serving: 2

Ingredients:

- 1 lb leg of lamb
- 1/2 cup bone broth
- 1/2 cup white wine
- 1 1/2 carrots, chopped
- 1 tbsp butter

Directions:

- Rub lamb with salt, pepper and oil. Brown it in a crock-pot set on high.
- Set it aside and throw in your veggies in the crock-pot, including onion and garlic to taste.

- When the veggies have acquired desired crispness, add in the bone broth and wine. Mix thoroughly. Submerge the lamb legs into the mixture. Cover and cook for four hours on high.

Nutrition:

- Calories - 782
- Fat - 45g
- Carbs - 7g
- Protein - 72g

CHILE PORK STEW

Serving: 16

Ingredients:

- 4 pounds pork loin roast, cut into 6 pieces
- 3 cans diced green chilies
- 3 poblano peppers, chopped
- 1 onion, diced
- 2 tablespoons chili powder
- 1 tablespoon paprika
- ¾ cup water
- Salt and pepper
- Cilantro, chopped

Directions:

- Place all ingredients except for the cilantro in the Instant Pot.
- Close the lid and press the Meat/Stew button.
- Adjust the cooking time to 40 minutes.

- Do natural pressure release.

Nutrition:

- Calories - 229
- Carbs - 2.4g
- Protein - 30.4g
- Fat - 10.3g

BEEF RATATOUILLE

Serving: 8

Ingredients:

- 1-pound beef
- 1 cup tomatoes
- 1 cup onion, diced
- 1 cup zucchini
- 1 cup eggplants, chopped
- 1 tablespoon garlic, sliced
- 1 tablespoon salt
- 1 teaspoon ground black pepper
- 1 teaspoon red pepper
- 1 teaspoon basil
- 1 cup fresh cilantro
- 3 tablespoons tomato sauce
- 2 tablespoons olive oil
- ½ cup water

Directions:

- Chop the tomatoes and zucchini. Put the prepared vegetables in the slow cooker.

- Add the chopped eggplants. Chop the beef and put it in a saute pan.
- Add the diced onion and olive oil. Roast the meat until it is golden brown. Add the tomato paste and roast it for 1 minute more.
- Then put the meat mixture into the slow cooker.
- Sprinkle the ratatouille mixture with the salt, sliced garlic, ground black pepper, red pepper, basil, and water.
- Chop the fresh cilantro and put in the slow cooker. Close the lid and cook the mixture on LOW for 9 hours.
- Open the slow cooker lid and stir the prepared dish. Add more salt if desired and Enjoy!

Nutrition:

- Calories - 128
- Fat - 6.7
- Carbs - 5
- Protein - 13

LAMB SHANKS WITH TOMATOES

Serving: 2

Ingredients:

- 1/3 tbsp tomato paste
- 1 x 400g tin diced tomatoes
- 1/3 tbsp sundried tomato pesto
- 1/3 cup beef stock
- 2 lb lamb shanks

Directions:

- Heat oil in a saucepan and cook onions until Add tomato paste and cook for another 2 minutes, stirring.

- Add diced tomatoes, sundried tomato pesto and beef stock. Bring to a boil. Put the lamb into the crock-pot and pour tomato sauce over. Cook for 8 hours on low.

Nutrition:

- Calories - 397
- Fat - 34g
- Carbs - 5g
- Protein - 29g
- Cholesterol - 110mg
- Sodium - 654mg

MOROCCAN LAMB

Serving: 8

Ingredients:

- 2-pound lamb shoulder
- 1 teaspoon cumin seeds
- 1 teaspoon ground cu minutes
- 1 teaspoon ground coriander
- 1 teaspoon celery root
- 1 teaspoon salt
- 1 teaspoon chili flakes
- 4 tablespoons tomato paste

- 3 tablespoons raisins
- 1 tablespoon dried apricots
- 5 cup water
- 1 cup onion, chopped

Directions:

- Combine the cumin seeds, ground cumin, ground coriander, celery root, salt, and chili flakes in a shallow bowl.
- After this, rub the lamb shoulder with the spice mixture and then brush with the tomato paste.
- Leave the meat for 10 minutes to marinate.
- Put the chopped onion in the slow cooker with the water.
- Then put the marinated meat in the slow cooker as well and close the lid.
- Cook the dish on LOW for 13 hours. Remove the meat from the liquid and serve it.

Nutrition:

- Calories - 195
- Fat - 9.6
- Carbs - 4.5
- Protein - 23

ITALIAN SHORT RIBS

Serving: 8

Ingredients:

- 2 tablespoons olive oil
- 1 ½ cups leeks, chopped
- 3 pounds short-ribs, bone in
- 1 teaspoon Italian seasoning
- Salt and pepper
- ½ cup dry white wine
- 1 ¼ cups pasta sauce

Directions:

- Press the Saute button on the Instant Pot.
- Heat the olive oil and saute the leeks.
- Add in the short ribs and the rest of the ingredients.
- Close the lid and press the Meat/Stew button.
- Adjust the cooking time to 60 minutes.
- Do natural pressure release.

Nutrition:

- Calories - 341
- Carbs - 33.3g
- Protein - 17.9g
- Fat - 15.1g

HERBED SPARE RIBS

Serving: 4

Ingredients:

- 15 oz pork spare ribs
- 1 teaspoon marjoram
- ½ teaspoon caraway seeds
- ½ teaspoon ground coriander
- ½ teaspoon dried oregano
- ½ teaspoon dried basil
- 1 tablespoon olive oil
- 1/3 cup water
- 1 teaspoon coconut oil

Directions:

- Rub the pork spare ribs with marjoram, caraway seeds, ground coriander, dried oregano, dried basil, and olive oil.
- Then place the spare ribs in the skillet and roast them for 5 minutes from each side over the medium heat.
- After this, Add water and coconut oil. Close the lid.
- Cook the spare ribs for 4.5 hours on High.

Nutrition:

- Calories - 201
- Fat - 15
- Carbs - 0.3
- Protein - 16.1

SWEET RIBS

Serving: 5

Ingredients:

- 2 lbs pork ribs, chopped
- 2 red bell peppers, sliced
- 1 green bell pepper, sliced
- 1 celery stalk, chopped
- ¼ cup soy sauce
- 1 tbsp apple cider
- 1 tbsp almond flour
- 3 tbsp oil
- Spices: 1 tsp salt
- ½ tsp dried basil
- 1 bay leaf
- 1 rosemary sprig, fresh

Directions:

- Place the ribs in the pot and pour in enough water to cover. Sprinkle with salt, add basil, bay leaf, and rosemary.
- Seal the lid.
- Set the steam release handle to the "Sealing" position and press the "MANUAL" button.
- Cook for 25 minutes on high pressure.
- When done, release the pressure naturally and open the lid. Remove the ribs from the pot and chill for a while.
- Grease the inner pot with oil and press the "Saute" button. Add bell peppers and celery stalks.

- Saute for 5-6 minutes, stirring constantly.
- Rub the ribs with soy sauce and add to the pot. Pour in the remaining soy sauce and about ¼ cup of water.
- Stir in the almond flour and simmer for 4-5 minutes.
- Press the "Cancel" button and serve immediately.

Nutrition:

- Calories - 367
- Fat - 15g
- Carbs - 5.8g
- Protein - 49.1g

ROSEMARY BEEF ROAST RECIPE

Serving: 6

Ingredients:

- 2 -pounds beef chuck roast; cut into large pieces
- 1 small onion; finely chopped
- 1 teaspoon balsamic vinegar
- 1 teaspoon olive oil
- 1/2 cup heavy cream
- 1 medium-sized red bell pepper; stripped
- 1 cup bone broth
- 3 garlic cloves; crushed
- 1 teaspoon black pepper; freshly ground.
- 1 teaspoon dried marjoram; ground.
- 1 teaspoon fresh rosemary; finely chopped
- 1/2 teaspoon dried parsley; ground.
- 1 teaspoon salt

Directions:

- Plug in your instant pot and grease the stainless steel insert with olive oil. Press the "SAUTE" button and add onions and garlic. Stir-fry for 3-4 minutes, or until Add meat and generously sprinkle with salt. Cook for 3-4 minutes on each side, or until lightly browned. Now; add all the remaining ingredients and spices. Close the lid and adjust the steam release handle. Press the "MANUAL" button and set the timer for 25 minutes. Cook on "HIGH" pressure
- When you hear the cooker's end signal, perform a quick release of the pressure and open the pot.

Nutrition:

- Calories - 619
- Fat - 46.7g
- Carbs - 3g
- Protein - 43.6g

BROWN RICE AND LAMB

Serving: 2

Ingredients:

- 12 ounces boneless lamb shoulder, cut in small cubes
- 2 tablespoons honey
- 2 tablespoons low sodium soy sauce
- 1 teaspoon olive oil
- 1 cup low sodium chicken broth

- ½ cup brown rice
- 1 scallion, white and green parts, sliced thin

Directions:

- In a mixing bowl, season the lamb with honey and soy sauce. Coat well.
- Grease the inside of the slow cooker with the olive oil.
- Add the lamb mixture, the broth, rice, and scallions. Mix well.
- Cover, and cook on LOW for 8 hours.
- Divide among serving bowls or plates, and enjoy!

Nutrition:

- Calories - 563
- Fat - 5 g
- Carbs - 53.8 g
- Protein - 48.6 g

PERNIL PORK

Serving: 2

Ingredients:

- ¾ tsp ground ancho chili pepper
- 2 tsp chopped fresh oregano
- 1 tsp white wine vinegar
- 3/8 lime, cut into wedges
- 3/8 (3 lb boneless pork loin roast

Directions:

- Prepare the seasoning: garlic, onion, salt and pepper to taste together with all of the other ingredients except the pork. Use a blender.
- Place the pork in a crock-pot and spread the mixture to it.
- Cook and cook for 6 hours on low.

Nutrition:

- Calories - 367
- Fat - 21g
- Carbs - 5.7g
- Protein - 37.6g
- Cholesterol - 108mg
- Sodium - 844mg

TACO SOUP WITH BEEF

Serving: 2

Ingredients:

- 1 cup cream cheese
- 1 cup cheddar cheese, shredded
- 1/2 cup tomato puree
- 2 lb ground beef, sauteed
- 3 1/2 cup chicken broth

Directions:

- Combine everything in a crock-pot. Add salt to taste.

- Cover and cook for 4 hours on low.

Nutrition:

- Calories - 569
- Fat - 41.2g
- Carbs - 4.8g
- Protein - 43g

CHILI PULLED PORK

Serving: 4

Ingredients:

- 1 teaspoon Erythritol
- ½ teaspoon ground black pepper
- 1 teaspoon chili flakes
- 1 teaspoon green chile, minced
- 1 teaspoon minced garlic
- 1 tablespoon mustard
- 1 teaspoon tomato paste
- 1-pound pork shoulder, boneless
- ½ cup of water
- 1 tablespoon coconut oil
- ½ teaspoon chili powder
- ¾ teaspoon turmeric

Directions:

- Put all ingredients from the list above in the crockpot.
- Close the lid and cook the pork for 10 hours on Low.

- After this, open the lid and shred the meat carefully with the help of 2 forks or use a knife and fork.
- Stir the pulled pork well.
- If you cook it in advance, cook the pulled pork for 20 minutes on High more. If you serve it immediately, no need to cook it anymore.

Nutrition:

- Calories - 379
- Fat - 28.6
- Carbs - 3.4
- Protein - 27.3

CROCK POT PORK RIBS

Serving: 6

Ingredients:

- 5 pounds pork ribs
- 2 tablespoons butter
- ½ cup beef stock
- 1 tablespoon crushed garlic
- 1 tablespoon onion powder
- 1 tablespoon thyme
- 1 tablespoon oregano
- ¼ teaspoon cayenne pepper
- ½ teaspoon black pepper
- 1 teaspoon allspice
- 1 teaspoon salt

Directions:

- Mix together all the spices to make a dry rub.
- With a sharp knife, poke slits in the back of the ribs.
- Generously rub the spices onto each side of the ribs.
- Place the ribs in the crock pot and add the butter and stock. Cover and cook for 6-8 hours.
- Serve hot.

Nutrition:

- Calories - 775
- Fat - 39 g
- Carbs - 8 g
- Protein - 89 g

HEARTY BEEF STEW

Serving: 2

Ingredients:

- 1 pound chuck beef
- 1 teaspoon salt
- 1/2 teaspoon black pepper
- 2 tablespoons butter
- 1 onion, chopped
- 2 carrots, sliced
- 1 celery stalk, sliced
- 1 teaspoon thyme
- 1/2 teaspoon rosemary
- 2 tablespoons flour

- 1 tablespoon tomato paste
- 2 cups beef broth
- 1/2 pound potatoes, chopped

Directions:

- Season the beef with salt and pepper. Melt the butter in the Instant Pot on Saute mode. Brown beef in butter. Remove to a plate.
- Add onion, carrots, and celery to the pot. Cook until onion is Add tomato paste, then beef broth and scrape off anything stuck to the bottom of the pot. Add potatoes and replace beef in pot.
- Close lid and set cooking time to 35 minutes on high pressure. Season to taste with salt and pepper.

Nutrition:

- Calories - 570
- Fat - 25.33 g
- Carbs - 33.68 g
- Protein - 53.64 g

GARLIC TERIYAKI BEEF

Serving: 4

Ingredients:

- 1 piece (2 lbs flank steak, sliced into ½-inch strips
- 2 cloves garlic, finely chopped
- For the teriyaki sauce: ¼ cup soy sauce

- ¼ cup maple syrup
- 1 tbsp raw honey
- 2 tbsp fish sauce, optional
- 1½ tsp ground or fresh ginger, optional

Directions:

- In a medium bowl, combine the soy sauce, maple syrup, honey, fish sauce, and ginger.
- Mix well.
- Add the sauce, steak strips and garlic to the Instant Pot, stir.
- Close and lock the lid. Select MANUAL and cook at HIGH pressure for 40 minutes.
- Once timer goes off, allow to
- Naturally Release
- for 10 minutes, then release any remaining pressure manually.
- Uncover the pot.
- Serve.

PORK POZOLE

Serving: 6

Ingredients:

- 1 ½ pound pork loin, chopped
- 1 cup edamame beans
- 1 teaspoon minced garlic
- 1 white onion, chopped
- 1 teaspoon ground cu minutes
- 1 teaspoon ground coriander
- 1 teaspoon salt

- 1 teaspoon paprika
- ½ teaspoon peppercorns
- 1 cup chicken stock
- 1/3 cup tomato sauce

Directions:

- Mix up together chicken stock, tomato sauce, peppercorns, paprika, salt, ground coriander, and cumin in the bowl and pour the mixture in the crockpot.
- Add chopped pork loin edamame beans, minced garlic, and chopped onion.
- Then close the lid and cook Pork Pozole for 4.5 hours on High.

Nutrition:

- Calories - 322
- Fat - 17.4
- Carbs - 5.7
- Protein - 34.5

SHORTCUT PORK POSOLE

Serving: 4

Ingredients:

- 1-pound pork shoulder, cut into chunks
- 1 onion, chopped
- 4 cloves of garlic, minced
- 25 ounces posole
- 1 can chipotle chilies

- 1 teaspoon dried oregano
- 2 teaspoon ground cu minutes
- ¾ cup water
- ¼ cup cilantro, chopped

Directions:

- Place all ingredients in the Instant Pot.
- Close the lid and press the Meat/Stew button.
- Adjust the cooking time to 30 minutes.
- Do natural pressure release.

Nutrition:

- Calories - 391
- Carbs - 8.3g
- Protein - 72g
- Fat - 3g

SIMPLE TOMATO PORK CHOPS

Serving: 2

Ingredients:

- 2 pork chops, with bones
- 1 cup cherry tomatoes
- 1 green bell pepper, sliced
- 1 small onion, finely chopped
- 4 tbsp olive oil
- 1 cup beef broth
- Spices: ½ tsp salt
- ½ tsp white pepper, freshly ground
- ¼ tsp garlic powder

Directions:

- Place the meat in the pot and season with salt. Pour in the broth and seal the lid. Set the steam release handle to the "Sealing" position and press the "MANUAL" button.
- Set the timer for 15 minutes on high pressure. When done, release the pressure naturally and open the lid.
- Remove the meat from the pot and Set aside.
- Now, press the "Saute" button and grease the inner pot with olive oil. Heat up and add onions and peppers. Sprinkle with some more salt. Cook for 5-6 minutes and then add cherry tomatoes. Pour in about ¼ cup of the broth and simmer for 10-12 minutes, stirring occasionally.
- Season with pepper and garlic powder. Optionally, add some red pepper flakes. Drizzle over
- pork chope and serve immediately.

Nutrition:

- Calories - 633
- Fat - 37g
- Carbs - 9.1g
- Protein - 63.6g

STUFFED LAMB WITH ONIONS

Serving: 9

Ingredients:

- 3-pounds lamb fillet
- 5 medium onions
- 3 garlic cloves
- 1 carrot
- 1 tablespoon ground black pepper
- 1 tablespoon olive oil
- ¼ cup sour cream
- 1 tablespoon salt
- 1 teaspoon rosemary

Directions:

- Peel the onions and slice them. Then peel the garlic cloves and mince them.
- Combine the sliced onions with the minced garlic.
- Make a "pocket" in the lamb fillet and fill it with the onion mixture. Peel the carrot and chop it then stuff it into the lamb as well.
- After this, secure the lamb fillet with toothpicks. Rub the lamb fillet with the ground
- black pepper, olive oil, sour cream salt, and rosemary.
- Wrap the prepared meat in the foil and put in the slow cooker. Cook the meat on HIGH for 6 hours. Then remove the meat from the slow cooker and discard the foil.
- Serve it!

Nutrition:

- Calories - 440
- Fat - 27.7
- Carbs - 8
- Protein - 38

WHISKEY BLUES STEAK

Serving: 6

Ingredients:

- 1 ½ pounds beef steak
- 1 teaspoon salt
- 2 teaspoons coarsely ground black pepper
- 3 cups zucchini, sliced thick
- ¼ cup butter
- 1 cup onions, sliced
- ¼ cup whiskey
- 2 cloves garlic, crushed and minced
- ½ cup blue cheese, crumbled

Directions:

- Season the steak with salt and black pepper.
- Place the sliced zucchini in the bottom of the slow cooker.
- Melt the butter in a skillet over medium-high heat. Add the steaks to the skillet and brown on both sides, approximately 2-4 minutes.
- Remove the steaks from the skillet and place them in the slow cooker.

- Add the onions to the skillet and saute until crisp tender, approximately 3-4 minutes.
- Add the whiskey and cook until reduced, 1-2 minutes, scraping the bottom of the skillet.
- Cover and cook on low for 6 hours, or until the steaks are cooked to the desired doneness, and are tender.
- Serve the steaks garnished with blue cheese.

Nutrition:

- Calories - 305.0
- Fat - 15.4 g
- Carbs - 6.1 g
- Protein - 29.2 g

GROUND BEEF SHAWARMA

Serving: 4

Ingredients:

- 1 lbs. Lean Ground Beef
- 1 cup Onions (cut to rubs)
- 1 cup Red Bell Peppers (cut into ¼ inch slices)
- 2 cups Cabbage (cut into ½ inch strips)
- 1 tsp Dried Oregano
- ½ tsp Cinnamon
- ¼ tsp Ground Allspice
- ¼ tsp Cayenne Pepper
- ½ tsp Cu minutes
- ½ tsp Ground Coriander Seeds
- 1 tsp Salt

Directions:

- Set the Instant Pot to "Saute" and add in it the ground beef. Lightly brown it while breaking down into smaller chunks, for around 2 minutes.
- Add all other ingredients and stir to combine.
- Place and lock the lid, and manually set the cooking time to 2 minutes at high pressure.
- Let naturally release the pressure for 5 minutes and then quick release it.
- Serve with tzatziki sauce.

Nutrition:

- Calories - 191
- Fat - 5g
- Carbs - 6g
- Protein - 25g

ASIAN BEEF SHORT RIBS

Serving: 6-8

Ingredients:

- 12 beef short ribs
- 2 tbsp olive oil
- ½ tsp salt
- ½ cup soy sauce
- 1 cup tomato paste
- 2 tbsp apple cider vinegar
- 4 cloves garlic, minced
- ¼ cup ginger root, diced
- 2 tbsp sriracha sauce

- ¼ cup raw honey

Directions:

- Select the SAUTe setting on the Instant Pot and heat the oil.
- Season the ribs with salt. Add to the pot and cook for 5 minutes on each side, until browned.
- Brown the short ribs in batches.
- Add the soy sauce, tomato paste, apple cider, garlic, ginger, sriracha and honey to the pot.
- Stir the mixture well, at the same time, deglaze the pot by scraping the bottom to remove all of the brown bits.
- Return the ribs to the pot.
- Press the CANCEL key to stop the SAUTe function.
- Close and lock the lid. Select MANUAL and cook at HIGH pressure for 35 minutes.
- Once timer goes off, allow to
- Naturally Release
- for 10-15 minutes, then release any remaining pressure manually.
- Open the lid.
- Serve with the gravy.

CILANTRO MEAT BOWL

Serving: 10

Ingredients:

- 1 cup cilantro
- 11 oz pork chops

- 8 oz beef brisket
- 1 tablespoon rosemary
- 1 teaspoon ground black pepper
- 1 teaspoon salt
- 1 teaspoon paprika
- 1 cup red onion
- 6 oz sweet yellow pepper, chopped
- 2 tablespoons lemon juice
- 1 teaspoon olive oil
- 1 teaspoon oregano
- 4 oz celery stalk, chopped
- 6 oz salsa
- ½ chili pepper

Directions:

- Wash the cilantro carefully and chop it. Chop the pork chops into cubes.
- Sprinkle the meat with the rosemary. Combine the chopped pork cubes with the beef brisket. Add ground black pepper, salt, paprika, lemon juice, and salsa and marinate it for 10 minutes.
- Then Add the red onion, chili pepper, chopped celery stalk, and sweet yellow pepper.
- Sprinkle the mixture with the oregano and olive oil. Cover the mixture with the chopped cilantro and close the lid.
- Cook the meat mixture on LOW for 13 hours.
- When the meat is cooked, stir it carefully with a wooden spoon. Serve the meat in bowls.
- Enjoy!

Nutrition:

- Calories - 134
- Fat - 7.4
- Carbs - 4.58
- Protein - 12

AMAZING APPLE PORK CHOPS

Serving: 8

Ingredients:

- 2 ½ pounds boneless pork chops
- 1 onion, chopped
- 3 garlic cloves, minced
- 1 teaspoon salt
- 1 teaspoon black pepper (ground
- 2 tablespoons olive oil
- 1 (28 ounce) can apple butter
- 1 cup applesauce

Directions:

- Season the pork chops with salt and pepper.
- Take your Instant Pot and open the top lid.
- Press "SAUTE" mode.
- Add the oil and heat it; stir-cook the chops until evenly brown.
- Set them aside.
- Add the onions to the pot and cook until Add the garlic and cook until fragrant, stirring constantly.
- Add the chops and remaining ingredients; gently stir.

- Close the top lid and seal the pressure valve.
- Press "MANUAL" setting with 20 minutes of cooking time and "HIGH" pressure mode.
- Press "NPR" function to release the pressure slowly in a natural way.
- Open the lid;

Nutrition:

- Calories - 394
- Fat - 9g
- Carbs - 39g
- Sodium - 514mg
- Protein - 31g

JUST PEACHY PORK CHOPS

Serving: 2

Ingredients:

- 2 pork loin chops
- 2 teaspoons olive oil
- ½ cup water
- 1 teaspoon soy sauce
- Pinch oregano, dried
- Pinch basil, dried
- Pinch thyme, dried
- Pinch red pepper flakes
- 1 cup fresh or canned peaches, sliced

Directions:

- Brown the pork chops with the olive oil in a medium-sized skillet.
- Arrange the chops in a slow cooker, saving any juices.
- In a mixing bowl, mix the cooking juices, tomato sauce, water, soy sauce, oregano, basil, thyme, and red pepper flakes. Pour the sauce over the chops and place the peaches on top of the arrangement.
- Cover, and cook for 5 hours on low. The pork should be fork tender.

Nutrition:

- Calories - 414
- Fat - 21 g
- Carbs - 23 g
- Protein - 34 g

SNACKS AND APPETIZERS

CHICKEN PATE

Serving: 8

Ingredients:

- 1 cup vegetable stock
- 1 ½ pounds chicken livers
- A pinch of salt and black pepper

- 2 garlic cloves, minced
- 3 tablespoons olive oil
- ½ cup lemon juice

Directions:

- In your slow cooker, combine all the ingredients except the oil and the lemon juice, cover and cook on low for 5 hours.

Nutrition:

- Calories - 193
- Fat - 11,2
- Carbs - 1,6
- Protein - 21

CHICKEN WINGS

Serving: 4

Ingredients:

- ¼ cup coconut aminos
- ¼ cup balsamic vinegar
- 2 garlic cloves, minced
- 2 tablespoon stevia
- 1 teaspoon sriracha sauce
- 3 tablespoons lime juice
- Zest from 1 lime, grated
- 1 teaspoon ginger powder
- 2 teaspoons sesame seeds
- 2 pounds chicken wings
- 2 tablespoons chives, chopped

Directions:

- In your slow cooker, mix aminos with vinegar, garlic, stevia, sriracha, lime juice, lime zest and ginger and stir well.
- Add chicken wings, toss well, cover and cook on High for 4 hours.
- Arrange chicken wings on a platter, sprinkle chives and sesame seeds on top and serve as a casual appetizer.
- Enjoy!

Nutrition:

- Calories - 212
- Fat - 3
- Carbs - 12
- Protein - 3

BROCCOLI CHEESE STICKS

Serving: 8

Ingredients:

- 1 cup broccoli, shredded
- 4 eggs, beaten
- 1 cup Cheddar cheese, shredded
- 1 tablespoon fresh dill, chopped
- 1 teaspoon butter, softened
- 1/3 cup almond flour
- 1 teaspoon salt

Directions:

- In the mixing bowl, mix up together beaten eggs, broccoli shred, shredded Cheddar cheese, butter, salt, and almond flour. You should get a soft homogenous mixture.
- Line the bottom of the crockpot with the baking paper.
- Close the lid and bake it for 2.5 hours on High.
- Then chill the cooked mixture very well and cut into the serving sticks.

Nutrition:

- Calories - 104
- Fat - 8
- Carbs - 1.6
- Protein - 7

BACON SKEWERS

Serving: 5

Ingredients:

- 1 cup ground pork
- ½ cup ground beef
- 4 oz bacon, sliced
- 1 tablespoon butter
- 1 teaspoon Italian seasoning
- 1 teaspoon salt
- 1 tablespoon crushed tomatoes
- ¼ cup heavy cream

Directions:

- In the mixing bowl, mix up together ground pork, ground beef, Italian seasoning, and salt.
- Then make the meatballs from the meat mixture.
- Wrap every meatball in the sliced bacon and string the meatballs on the skewers.
- Mix up together crushed tomatoes with cream and pour the liquid in the crockpot.
- Add the prepared meatball skewers and cook appetizer for 3 hours on High.

Nutrition:

- Calories - 380
- Fat - 28.9
- Carbs - 0.8
- Protein - 27.3

UNIQUE PARTY FOOD

Serving: 4

Ingredients:

- 1 pound asparagus spears
- 8-ounce sliced prosciutto

Directions:

- Wrap the prosciutto slices around asparagus spears.
- In the bottom of Instant Pot, arrange a steamer basket and pour 2 cups of water.

- Place the carrots into the steamer basket.
- Arrange any extra un-wrapped spears in the bottom of the steamer basket in a single layer.
- Place prosciutto-wrapped asparagus on top in a single layer.
- Secure the lid and place the pressure valve to "Seal" position.
- Select "MANUAL" and cook under "High Pressure" for about 2-3 minutes.
- Select the "Cancel" and carefully do a Natural release.
- Remove the lid and serve warm

Nutrition:

- Calories - 105
- Fat - 3.3g
- Carbs - 1.32 g
- Protein - 14.4g

PORK LETTUCE FOLDS

Serving: 4

Ingredients:

- 1 cup ground pork
- 1 teaspoon tomato paste
- 1 teaspoon chili flakes
- ¼ white onion, diced
- 8 lettuce leaves
- ¼ cup heavy cream
- 1 teaspoon coconut oil
- ½ teaspoon salt

Directions:

- Put the ground pork, tomato paste, chili flakes, onion, coconut oil, and salt in the crockpot.
- Add heavy cream and mix up the mixture very carefully.
- Close the lid and cook ground pork for 4 hours on High.
- Then mix up the cooked ground pork very carefully and chill for 10-15 minutes.
- Place 2 lettuce leaves to get the cross.
- Put the small amount of ground pork in the center of lettuce cross and fold it.
- Repeat the same steps with remaining lettuce leaves.

Nutrition:

- Calories - 273
- Fat - 20.2
- Carbs - 1.4
- Protein - 20.5

BRAISED PULLED HAM

Serving: 7

Ingredients:

- 18 oz ham
- 1 teaspoon onion powder
- 1 teaspoon garlic powder
- 1 teaspoon chili flakes
- 1 tablespoon avocado oil

- 1 tablespoon mustard
- 1 teaspoon minced garlic
- ½ cup of water
- 1 teaspoon tomato sauce
- ½ teaspoon salt

Directions:

- Rub ham with onion powder, garlic powder, chili flakes, avocado oil, mustard, minced garlic, tomato sauce, and salt.
- Close the lid and cook the ham for 12 hours on Low.
- When the ham is cooked, shred it with the help of 2 forks.
- Cook pulled ham for 30 minutes on high.

Nutrition:

- Calories - 132
- Fat - 7
- Carbs - 4.2
- Protein - 12.7

MEDITERRANEAN OLIVE SPREAD

Serving: 6

Ingredients:

- 1 cup black olives, pitted
- 1 cup kalamata olives, pitted
- 1 cup green olives, pitted
- 5 garlic cloves, minced

- A pinch of black pepper
- 2 tablespoons olive oil
- ½ cup vegetable stock
- 1 teaspoon lemon zest

Directions:

- In your slow cooker, combine all the ingredients, cover and cook on low for 2 hours and 30 minutes.

Nutrition:

- Calories - 154
- Fat - 15,8
- Carbs - 2,8
- Protein - 0,8

SPAGHETTI FRITTERS

Serving: 10

Ingredients:

- 10 oz pasta, cooked
- ½ cup bread crumbs
- 4 oz Romano cheese
- 4 teaspoons sesame oil
- 1 teaspoon paprika
- 1 teaspoon ground black pepper
- 1 teaspoon salt
- 3 eggs

Directions:

- Chop the pasta gently and combine with the bread crumbs.
- Beat the eggs in the bowl and whisk them well. Then add the whisked eggs to the pasta mixture. After this, add paprika, bread crumbs, ground black pepper, and salt and mix.
- Then spray your hands with the sesame oil so the dough doesn't stick as you form the small fritters from the dough.
- Place the uncooked fritters in the slow cooker and close the slow cooker lid.
- Cook the fritters on HIGH for 2 hours.
- After this, flip the fritters over and cook the fritters for 1 hour more on HIGH. Remove the fritters from the slow cooker and chill little.
- Enjoy!

Nutrition:

- Calories - 177
- Fat - 10.1
- Carbs - 12.55
- Protein - 9

CAULIFLOWER HUMMUS

Serving: 4

Ingredients:

- 4 tablespoons sesame seed paste
- ¼ cup vegetable stock

- 1 cauliflower head, florets separated
- 5 tablespoons olive oil
- 4 tablespoons lime juice
- 1 teaspoon garlic powder
- A pinch of salt and black pepper

Directions:

- In your slow cooker, combine all the ingredients except the sesame seed paste and the lime juice. Mix together, cover and cook on low for 4 hours.

Nutrition:

- Calories - 224
- Fat - 22,2
- Carbs - 7,2
- Protein - 3,1

BEEF BITES

Serving: 10

Ingredients:

- 2 pounds beef, cubed
- 1 red chili pepper, chopped
- 1/5 cup tomato sauce

Directions:

- In your slow cooker, combine all the ingredients, cover and cook on low for 8 hours.
- Divide into bowls and serve warm.

Nutrition:

- Calories - 170
- Fat - 5,7
- Carbs - 0,3
- Protein - 27,6

CHICKEN WINGS

Serving: 4

Ingredients:

- ¼ cup coconut aminos
- ¼ cup balsamic vinegar
- 2 garlic cloves, minced
- 2 tablespoon stevia
- 1 teaspoon sriracha sauce
- 3 tablespoons lime juice
- Zest from 1 lime, grated
- 1 teaspoon ginger powder
- 2 teaspoons sesame seeds
- 2 pounds chicken wings
- 2 tablespoons chives, chopped

Directions:

- In your slow cooker, mix aminos with vinegar, garlic, stevia, sriracha, lime juice, lime zest and ginger and stir well.
- Add chicken wings, toss well, cover and cook on High for 4 hours.

- Arrange chicken wings on a platter, sprinkle chives and sesame seeds on top and serve as a casual appetizer.
- Enjoy!

Nutrition:

- Calories - 212
- Fat - 3
- Carbs - 12
- Protein - 3

SEMI-SWEET MEATBALLS

Serving: 8

Ingredients:

- 2 tablespoons soy sauce
- 1 tablespoon apple cider vinegar
- 1 teaspoon ground black pepper
- 3 tablespoons sugar
- 1 teaspoon cilantro
- ½ cup tomato sauce
- 1 egg
- 2 tablespoons bread crumbs
- 1 teaspoon minced garlic
- 1 teaspoon onion powder
- 1 teaspoon salt
- 1 teaspoon ground white pepper
- 10 oz ground beef
- 3 tablespoons fresh parsley

Directions:

- Beat the egg in the bowl. Add the bread crumbs, ground beef, ground black pepper, salt, onion powder, and minced garlic.
- Mix carefully. Combine the soy sauce, apple cider vinegar, ground white pepper, sugar, tomato sauce, and fresh parsley.
- Mix and place in the slow cooker bowl.
- Then form the meatballs from the ground beef mixture and Close the slow cooker lid and cook the dish for 7 hours on LOW. Serve the meatballs with the sauce.
- Enjoy!

Nutrition:

- Calories - 201
- Fat - 13
- Carbs - 12
- Protein - 8

SPICY PECANS

Serving: 5

Ingredients:

- 1 pound pecans, halved
- 2 tablespoons olive oil
- 1 teaspoon basil, dried
- 1 tablespoon chili powder
- 1 teaspoon oregano, dried
- ¼ teaspoon garlic powder

- 1 teaspoon thyme, dried
- ½ teaspoon onion powder
- A pinch of cayenne pepper

Directions:

- In your slow cooker, mix pecans with oil, basil, chili powder, oregano, garlic powder, onion powder, thyme and cayenne and toss to coat.
- Cover and cook on High for 15 minutes.
- Switch slow cooker to Low and cook for 2 hours.
- Divide into bowls and serve as a snack.
- Enjoy!

Nutrition:

- Calories - 78
- Fat - 3
- Carbs - 9
- Protein - 2

GARLIC BRUSSELS SPROUTS

Serving: 4-

Ingredients:

- ¼ cup mayo
- 1 pound Brussels sprouts
- ¼ cup sour cream
- ¾ cup mozzarella, shredded
- 2 garlic cloves
- ¼ cup parmesan
- 4 ounces cream cheese

- ½ teaspoon thyme
- 1 tablespoon olive oil

Directions:

- Preheat an oven to 400 degrees F.
- Coat the sprouts with the oil, pepper, and salt. Add the garlic.
- Bake the sprouts for 20-30 minutes. Flip halfway.
- Remove skins from garlic, then mix everything in your pot.
- Close the lid and lock. Ensure that you have sealed the valve to avoid leakage.
- Press "Slow cook" mode from available cooking settings and set cooking time to 3-4 hours. Instant Pot will start cooking the ingredients after a few minutes.
- After the timer reads zero, press "Cancel" and quick release pressure.
- Carefully remove the lid and serve the prepared keto dish warm!

Nutrition:

- Calories - 252
- Fat - 16.5g
- Carbs - 2g
- Protein - 15g

OREGANO CHEESE DIP

Serving: 4

Ingredients:

- ½ cup Cheddar cheese, shredded
- 2 oz Monterey Jack cheese, shredded
- 1 tablespoon dried oregano
- 2 tablespoon butter
- 1 teaspoon smoked paprika
- 2 oz Swiss cheese, grated
- ¼ cup coconut cream

Directions:

- Put all ingredients from the list above in the crockpot.
- Close the lid and cook the dip of High for 2 hours.

Nutrition:

- Calories - 254
- Fat - 22.4
- Carbs - 2.9
- Protein - 11.4

TRADITIONAL BRITISH SCOTCH EGGS

Serving: 4

Ingredients:

- 4 large organic eggs
- 1 pound gluten-free country style ground sausage
- 1 tbsp. olive oil

Directions:

- In the bottom of Instant Pot, arrange a steamer basket and pour 1 cup of water.
- Place eggs into the steamer basket.
- Secure the lid and place the pressure valve to "Seal" position.
- Select "MANUAL" and cook under "High Pressure" for about 6 minutes.
- Select the "Cancel" and carefully do a Quick release.
- Remove the lid and After cooling, peel the eggs.
- Divide sausage into 4 equal sized portions.
- Flat each portion into an oval-shaped patty.
- Place 1 egg in the middle of each patty and gently, mold the meat around the egg.
- Remove the basket from Instant Pot and drain the water.
- Place the oil in the Instant Pot and select "Saute". Then add the scotch eggs and garlic and cook until golden brown from all sides.
- Arrange a steamer trivet in the bottom of Instant Pot. Add 1 cup of water in Instant Pot.

- Place the scotch eggs on top of the trivet.
- Secure the lid and place the pressure valve to "Seal" position.
- Select "MANUAL" and cook under "High Pressure" for about 6 minutes.
- Select the "Cancel" and carefully do a Quick release.
- Remove the lid and serve immediately.

Nutrition:

- Calories - 486
- Fat - 40.6g
- Carbs - 0.1g
- Protein - 28.3g

TOMATO AND AVOCADO SALSA

Serving: 4

Ingredients:

- 4 cups tomatoes, cubed
- 2 teaspoons capers, chopped
- 2 avocados, peeled, pitted and cubed
- 4 garlic cloves, minced
- 2 teaspoons balsamic vinegar
- 2 tablespoon fresh chopped cilantro
- A pinch of salt and black pepper

Directions:

- In your slow cooker, combine all the ingredients except the cilantro and the avocados. Cover and cook on low for 6 hours.
- Divide into bowls, add the cilantro and the avocados, toss and serve.

Nutrition:

- Calories - 243
- Fat - 20
- Carbs - 16,7
- Protein - 3,7

CHESTNUT DIP

Serving: 4

Ingredients:

- 1 cup almond milk
- 2 tablespoons lime juice
- 2 garlic cloves, chopped
- 28 ounces water chestnuts, drained
- 8 ounces spinach
- Black pepper to the taste

Directions:

- In your slow cooker, combine all the ingredients, cover and cook on high for 2 hours.
- Blend using an immersion blender, divide into bowls and serve as a dip.

Nutrition:

- Calories - 460
- Fat - 15,6
- Carbs - 75,6
- Protein - 7,6

CHILI SCROLLS

Serving: 8

Ingredients:

- 7 oz puff pastry
- 2 chili pepper
- 1 tablespoon tomato sauce
- 1 tablespoon butter
- 1 egg yolk
- 1 teaspoon salt
- 1 teaspoon minced garlic
- 1 tablespoon mayo
- 1 teaspoon olive oil

Directions:

- Roll the puff pastry with the rolling pin.
- Remove the seeds from the chili peppers and chop them into the tiny pieces.
- Combine the chopped chili peppers with the tomato sauce and salt.
- Add minced garlic and mayo.
- Whisk the egg yolk and spread the rolled puff pastry with the chopped chili mixture and roll it

up. Cut the dough into pieces (scrolls. Brush every scroll with the whisked egg.
- Cover the slow cooker bowl with the parchment and place the scrolls there.
- Close the slow cooker lid and cook the chili scrolls for 4 hours on HIGH.
- When the dish is cooked, cool slightly then serve!

Nutrition:

- Calories - 169
- Fat - 12.1
- Carbs - 13.02
- Protein - 3

DESSERTS

COCONUT CAKE WITH CHOCOLATE TOPPING

Serving: 8

Ingredients:

- 1 cup coconut flour
- 2/3 cup almond meal
- 1 tsp baking powder
- 1 cup coconut oil
- 2 large eggs
- ¼ cup swerve
- 1 tsp vanilla extract
- ¼ cup cocoa powder, unsweetened

- 1 tsp stevia powder
- 1 cup whipped cream

Directions:

- In a large mixing bowl, combine coconut flour, almond meal, baking powder, and swerve. Crack eggs and beat well on medium speed. Now add 2/3 cup coconut oil and continue to mix until fully incorporated.
- Brush a 7-inches springform pan with some oil and dust with some cocoa powder. Plug in your instant pot and pour in 1 cup of water. Set the trivet at the bottom and put the wrapped springform on top. Seal the lid and set the steam release handle to the "SEALING" position.
- Set the timer for 25 minutes.
- When done, press the "CANCEL" button and perform a quick release by moving the
- pressure valve to the "VENTING" position.
- Open the lid and gently remove the pan. Cool to a room temperature.
- Meanwhile, press the "SAUTE" button on your instant pot. Add the remaining coconut oil, vanilla extract, stevia powder, and cocoa powder. Stir vigorously and add whipped cream. Cook for 1 minute. Press the "CANCEL" button again and remove the chocolate sauce from the instant pot.
- Drizzle the chilled cake with the chocolate sauce and refrigerate for 1 hour before serving.

Nutrition:

- Calories - 426
- Fat - 39.3g
- Carbs - 7.3g
- Protein - 6.6g

SWEET POTATO AND CINNAMON PATTIES

Serving: 4

Ingredients:

- 1 small sweet potato; cubed
- 1/2 cup Mascarpone
- 1/2 cup almond flour
- 1 tablespoon psyllium husk powder
- 3 tablespoon granulated stevia
- 1/4 cup flaxseed meal
- 3 tablespoon coconut oil; softened
- 1/2 teaspoon cinnamon powder
- 1 teaspoon vanilla extract

Directions:

- Plug in the instant pot and add potatoes. Pour in enough water to cover and seal the lid. Set the steam release handle and cook for 3 minutes on the "MANUAL" mode.
- When done, perform a quick pressure release and open the lid.
- Remove potatoes from the pot and drain. Cool for a while and a

- food processor along with the remaining ingredients. Process until smooth
- Now press the "SAUTE" button and grease the inner pot with some oil. Add about 1/4
- cup of the potato mixture and cook for 3-4 minutes on one side
- Gently turn over and continue to cook for another 2 minutes
- Repeat the process with the remaining mixture
- Optionally, sprinkle with some granulated stevia before serving

Nutrition:

- Calories - 213
- Fat - 18.1g
- Carbs - 4g
- Protein - 5.8g

SWEET APPLE BUTTER

Serving: 6

Ingredients:

- 1-pound sweet apples
- 6 oz white sugar
- 2 oz cinnamon stick
- ¼ teaspoon salt
- ¼ teaspoon ground ginger

Directions:

- Peel the apples and chop the fruits into the small pieces.
- Then put the apples in the slow cooker bowl. Sprinkle the fruits with the white sugar and add the cinnamon stick. After this, add salt and ground ginger.
- Do not stir the mixture and close the slow cooker. Cook the apples on HIGH for 3 hours stirring every 30 minutes. Blend the apples until you get s buttery texture.
- Close the slow cooker lid again and cook it on LOW for 3 hours more. When the apple butter is cooked, it has light brown color. Chill the apple butter well and enjoy it.

Nutrition:

- Calories - 222
- Fat - 14.1
- Carbs - 27.15
- Protein - 3

ASIAN MEATBALLS

Serving: 4

Ingredients:

- 1 cup ground beef
- 1 teaspoon salt
- ½ teaspoon ground black pepper
- 1 egg yolk

- 1 teaspoon Erythritol
- 2 tablespoons apple cider vinegar
- 1 teaspoon lime juice
- ¼ teaspoon lime zest
- 1/3 cup crushed tomatoes
- 1 teaspoon sesame seeds
- 1 teaspoon olive oil

Directions:

- Make the meatballs: mix up together ground beef, salt, ground black pepper, and egg yolk.
- When the mixture is smooth, make the small meatballs with the help of the fingertips and In the separated bowl, mix up together Erythritol, apple cider vinegar, lime juice, lime zest, crushed tomatoes, olive oil, and sesame seeds.
- Pour the mixture over the meatballs and close the crockpot lid.
- Cook the meatballs for 2.5 hours on High.

Nutrition:

- Calories - 103
- Fat - 6.8
- Carbs - 3.5
- Protein - 7.9

CARROT FRITTERS

Serving: 12

Ingredients:

- 2 large carrots
- 4 oz broccoli
- 1 tablespoon cream cheese
- ¼ cup flour
- 1 teaspoon salt
- 1 teaspoon ground black pepper
- 1 teaspoon paprika
- 1 teaspoon butter
- 4 tablespoons fresh cilantro, chopped
- 1 egg
- 3 oz celery stalk

Directions:

- Peel the carrots and grate them. Then put the grated carrot in the mixing bowl.
- Crack the egg into the bowl and add the cream cheese, flour, salt, ground black pepper, paprika, fresh cilantro, and mix it gently.
- Then grind celery stalk and add to the carrot mixture too.
- Chop the broccoli and add it to the mixture. Mix into a smooth dough. Butter the slow cooker bowl. Form the fritters from the carrot mass and put them in the slow cooker.
- Close the lid and cook the dish for 3 hours on HIGH. After this, flip the fritters and cook for 1 hour on HIGH. Serve the snack immediately.

Nutrition:

- Calories - 37
- Fat - 1.6
- Carbs - 4.22
- Protein - 2

CHILI SCROLLS

Serving: 8

Ingredients:

- 7 oz puff pastry
- 2 chili pepper
- 1 tablespoon tomato sauce
- 1 tablespoon butter
- 1 egg yolk
- 1 teaspoon salt
- 1 teaspoon minced garlic
- 1 tablespoon mayo
- 1 teaspoon olive oil

Directions:

- Roll the puff pastry with the rolling pin.
- Remove the seeds from the chili peppers and chop them into the tiny pieces.
- Combine the chopped chili peppers with the tomato sauce and salt.
- Add minced garlic and mayo.
- Whisk the egg yolk and spread the rolled puff pastry with the chopped chili mixture and roll it

up. Cut the dough into pieces (scrolls. Brush every scroll with the whisked egg.
- Cover the slow cooker bowl with the parchment and place the scrolls there.
- Close the slow cooker lid and cook the chili scrolls for 4 hours on HIGH.
- When the dish is cooked, cool slightly then serve!

Nutrition:

- Calories - 169
- Fat - 12.1
- Carbs - 13.02
- Protein - 3

PUMPKIN PIE PANCAKES

Serving: 4

Ingredients:

- 1 cup pumpkin puree
- 3 large eggs
- 2 tbsp. swerve
- ¾ cup almond flour
- 4 tbsp. almond milk, unsweetened
- 1 tsp pumpkin pie seasoning
- ¼ tsp salt
- 2 tsp baking powder

Directions:

- In a large mixing bowl, combine eggs, swerve, pumpkin pie seasoning, and almond milk. With a whisking attachment on, beat well on high speed. Gradually add flour, salt, baking powder, and pumpkin pie seasoning.
- Continue to mix for another 2 minutes.
- Finally, add the pumpkin puree and mix well again.
- Plug in your instant pot and press the "SAUTE" button. Grease the stainless steel insert with some oil and heat up. Add about ¼ cup of the batter and cook for 3 minutes.
- When done, gently remove from your instant pot and top with some blueberries, raspberries, or almonds.

Nutrition:

- Calories - 143
- Fat - 10g
- Carbs - 5.7g
- Protein - 6.9g

MAPLE APRICOT PIE

Serving: 4

Ingredients:

- 4 cups chopped apricots
- ½ tablespoon ground cinnamon
- 1 ½ cups coconut flour

- 1/2 teaspoon baking soda
- 3 tablespoons lemon juice
- ¼ cup coconut oil, melted
- 4 eggs, whisked
- 3½ tablespoons maple syrup
- ¼ teaspoon vanilla extract
- 2 tablespoons coconut milk

Directions:

- In a bowl, combine the flour with the baking soda, lemon juice, eggs, coconut oil, vanilla extract, half of the maple syrup and the milk and stir until a smooth batter forms.
- In a separate bowl, combine the apricots with the rest of the maple syrup and the cinnamon, stir spread them in your slow cooker.
- Drop spoonfuls of the eggs mix over the apricots, cover, cook on low for 4 hours, divide into bowls and serve.

Nutrition:

- Calories - 502
- Fat - 21,8
- Carbs - 73,7
- Protein - 8,6

TORTILLA PORK BITES

Serving: 2

Ingredients:

- 2 keto tortillas
- 2 lettuce leaves
- 1/3 cup ground pork
- 1 teaspoon tomato paste
- ½ teaspoon ground coriander
- ¾ teaspoon ground nutmeg
- ¾ teaspoon salt
- 3 tablespoons butter

Directions:

- Put ground pork, tomato paste, ground coriander, ground nutmeg, salt, and butter in the crockpot.
- Close the lid and cook meat on High for 5 hours.
- Then mix up the mixture well.
- Fill the lettuce leaves with ground pork mixture.
- Put the filled lettuce leaves on the keto tortillas and fold them. Secure the tortilla bites with the toothpicks.

Nutrition:

- Calories - 390
- Fat - 32.4
- Carbs - 5.1
- Protein - 19.8

COCOA BARS

Serving: 8

Ingredients:

- 1 cup cocoa
- 1 cup flour
- 1 cup butter
- 1 teaspoon baking powder
- 1 tablespoon lime juice
- 2 teaspoons lemon zest
- ½ cup pecan, crushed
- ¼ teaspoon olive oil
- 2 tablespoons dried apricots, chopped

Directions:

- Combine the cocoa, flour, baking powder, lemon zest, crushed pecans, and chopped dried apricots in the bowl.
- Melt the butter and add the melted butter and lime juice to the cocoa mixture. Make a soft but non-sticky dough and knead it with your hands.
- Then wrap the dough in the plastic wrap and put it in the fridge for 10 minutes. When the dough is little bit firm, remove it from the fridge and roll in the shape of the slow cooker bowl surface. Cover the slow cooker bowl with baking paper.
- Put the prepared cocoa dough in the slow cooker and cut it into the bars with the help of the knife. Then close the slow cooker lid.
- Cook the cocoa bars for 3.5 hours on HIGH.

- Check if the cocoa bars are cooked and remove them from the slow cooker gently to not damage them. Serve the cocoa bars warm with milk. Enjoy!

Nutrition:

- Calories - 338
- Fat - 29.2
- Carbs - 21.75
- Protein - 4

SIMPLE CAKE

Serving: 10

Ingredients:

- 1 cup almond flour
- ½ cup coconut sugar
- ½ teaspoons baking soda
- 3 tablespoons lemon juice
- 3 eggs, whisked
- 4 tablespoons coconut oil, melted
- ¾ teaspoon vanilla extract
- 2/3 cup almond milk
- 1/3 cup cocoa powder
- 2 tablespoons cocoa butter

Directions:

- In a bowl, mix all the ingredients and stir well.

- Pour this into a slow cooker lined with parchment paper and cook on low for 2 hours and 30 minutes.
- Leave the cake to cool down, slice and serve it.

Nutrition:

- Calories - 194
- Fat - 15,7
- Carbs - 13,3
- Protein - 3,2

COCOA BALLS

Serving: 8

Ingredients:

- 2 cups coconut flour
- 1 cup coconut sugar
- ¾ cup cocoa powder
- 1/2 teaspoon baking soda
- 2 tablespoons lemon juice
- 2 eggs, whisked
- 1 cup coconut milk
- ½ cup coconut oil, melted
- 2 teaspoons vanilla extract

Directions:

- In a bowl, combine all the ingredients except the coconut oil.
- Mix well.

- Add the coconut oil to your slow cooker then add the cookie mix. Spread the cookie mix in the pan, cover and cook on low for 4 hours. Take
- spoonful's
- of the mix and shape into balls and serve cold.

Nutrition:

- Calories - 333
- Fat - 23,5
- Carbs - 33,4
- Protein - 4,1

PECAN BROWNIES

Serving: 8

Ingredients:

- 6 oz cocoa powder
- 3 oz dark chocolate
- 1 teaspoon baking powder
- 1 tablespoon lemon juice
- ¼ cup pecan
- 1 cup flour
- ½ cup skim milk
- 2 eggs
- 1 tablespoon butter
- 1 teaspoon vanilla extract

Directions:

- Crush the dark chocolate carefully. Combine the crushed dark chocolate with the cocoa powder

and baking soda. Crush the pecan and add them to the chocolate mixture.
- Then add flour and stir it. Beat the eggs in a separate bowl. Whisk them with the skim milk and vanilla extract.
- Melt the butter and add it to the skim milk mixture. Combine the dry mass with the
- liquid mass together.
- Then cover the slow cooker bowl with parchment.
- Put the chocolate dough in the slow cooker and flatten it. Close the lid and cook the brownie for 5 hours on LOW.
- When the pecan brownie is cooked, remove it gently from the slow cooker and let it chill well.
- Cut it into the serving pieces. Serve it!

Nutrition:

- Calories - 280
- Fat - 11.4
- Carbs - 35.26
- Protein - 9

MONKEY BREAD

Serving: 6

Ingredients:

- 1 teaspoon cinnamon
- 1 cup brown sugar
- ¼ cup butter, melted
- 1 tube biscuits like Pillsbury Biscuits

Directions:

- Break biscuits into the pre-cut pieces.
- Mix the brown sugar and cinnamon.
- Dip biscuit pieces into melted butter.
- Put buttered biscuit into a bowl of cinnamon and brown sugar until fully coat.
- Place the pieces into slow cooker until you have all of the pieces layered in the slow cooker.
- Pour extra brown sugar and cinnamon on top.
- Cook on LOW for 2 hours.
- Serve.

Nutrition:

- Calories - 368
- Fat - 9.2 g
- Carbs - 68.1 g
- Protein - 5.1 g

VANILLA MINT CAKE

Serving: 6

Ingredients:

- 1/2 cup almond flour
- 5 large eggs yolks
- 3 tablespoon granulated stevia
- 1/2 teaspoon vanilla extract
- 1/4 cup butter
- 1 tablespoon unsweetened cocoa powder
- 1/2 teaspoon baking powder
- 1/4 teaspoon salt

- For the icing: 1 teaspoon mint extract
- 1 tablespoon shredded dark chocolate; 80% cocoa
- 2 tablespoon butter; softened
- 5 large egg whites
- 1/4 cup raspberries; for topping

Directions:

- First, line a fitting springform pan for your instant pot with some parchment paper. Grease the inside walls with some cooking spray and set aside.
- Combine almond flour, granulated stevia, cocoa powder, baking powder, and salt in a large bowl. Using a kitchen spatula, stir to combine, Set aside.
- In a separate mixing bowl, combine butter, egg yolks, and vanilla extract. Beat using a stand mixer for 3 minutes
- Now; stir in the wet ingredients into dry ingredients. Continue to beat until all well incorporated. Pour the mixture into previously prepared pan
- Plug in the instant pot and pour 1 cup of water in the stainless steel insert. Set the trivet on the bottom and place the pan on top
- Securely lock the lid and adjust the steam release handle. Press the "MANUAL" button and set the timer for 30 minutes. Cook on "HIGH" pressure.
- Meanwhile, combine icing ingredients in a large bowl. Whisk for 3.4 minutes, or until smooth and creamy. Fill the pipping bag with this mixture and set aside.

- When you hear the cooker's end signal, perform a quick pressure release and open the pot. Decorate the cake with icing and top with raspberries

Nutrition:

- Calories - 274
- Fat - 24.1g
- Carbs - 3.2g
- Protein - 10.1g

APPLE LEMON PIE

Serving: 10

Ingredients:

- 2 small Granny Smith's apples, peeled and thinly sliced
- 1 cup coconut flour
- ½ cup almond flour
- 1 tsp baking powder
- ½ tsp salt
- 1 tbsp. lemon juice, freshly squeezed
- 1 tsp lemon extract, sugar-free
- 1 tbsp. instant gelatin
- 3 tbsp. coconut oil, melted

Directions:

- Combine apples, lemon extract, and lemon juice in a large bowl. Mix until apple slices are well coated. Set aside.

- Now, combine all dry ingredients in a large bowl and mix until combined. Add all wet ingredients and mix with a kitchen spatula until dough is formed. Using your hands, flatten the dough into a circle crust. Place the dough on the top of the apple mixture.
- Set aside.
- Plug in your instant pot and pour in 2 cups of water. Position a trivet in the stainless steel insert. Place the pan on top and securely lock the lid. Adjust the steam release handle and set the timer for 20 minutes.
- Cook on high pressure.
- When done, press "Cancel" button and turn off the pot.
- Release the pressure naturally.
- Open the pot and let it chill for a while. Once cooled, turn the pan upside down and remove the parchment paper.
- Cut into slices and serve immediately.

Nutrition:

- Calories - 132
- Fat - 6.9g
- Carbs - 7g
- Protein - 3.2g

BREWED COFFEE PIE

Serving: 8

Ingredients:

- 4 tablespoons brewed coffee
- 2 cup flour
- 2 eggs
- 1 cup almond milk
- 1 teaspoon baking powder
- 1 tablespoon instant coffee
- 1 tablespoon cocoa powder
- 1 teaspoon lemon juice
- 1 cup sour cream
- 4 tablespoons sugar
- ½ cup sugar, brown
- 2 kiwi

Directions:

- Beat the eggs in a mixing bowl. Add the brewed coffee and baking powder. Then add the lemon juice, sour cream, and brown sugar. Mix well.
- Cover the slow cooker bowl with parchment. Meanwhile, combine the cocoa powder and instant coffee together. Stir the dry mixture. Peel the kiwi and mash them with the help of a fork.
- When the pie is cooked, remove it from the slow cooker and spread the surface with the smashed kiwi mixture. Then sprinkle it with the instant coffee mixture.
- Cut the pie into pieces and serve it immediately.

Nutrition:

- Calories - 261
- Fat - 6.2
- Carbs - 44.7
- Protein - 7

CRUSTLESS BEEF PIZZA

Serving: 2

Ingredients:

- 3/4 cup pizza sauce
- 1 lb ground beef, browned
- 1 cup mozzarella cheese
- pizza toppings of your choice (pepperoni, mushrooms, peppers, etc.

Directions:

- Mix the ground beef and mozzarella in the crockpot then spread evenly across the bottom.
- Top it with pizza sauce then put the desired toppings.
- Cover and cook for 4 hours on low.

Nutrition:

- Calories - 178
- Fat - 9.8 g
- Carbs - 4/8 g
- Protein - 10.4 g

- Serving suggestions: Serve with some Parmesan cheese.
- Tip: You will know the recipe is cooked when a toothpick comes out clean when the cake is poked.

RASPBERRY MUFFINS WITH CHOCOLATE TOPPING

Serving: 6

Ingredients:

- 1 cup fresh raspberries
- 1/4 cup coconut butter; melted
- 1 cup almond flour
- 1/4 cup granulated stevia
- 2 large eggs
- 1 teaspoon vanilla extract
- 1/4 cup whole milk
- 1 teaspoon baking powder
- 1/4 teaspoon salt
- For the topping: 1/4 teaspoon cinnamon; ground.
- 1/4 cup dark chocolate chips; melted
- 1/4 cup butter

Directions:

- In a large mixing bowl, combine almond flour, stevia, baking powder, and salt. Mix until combined and set aside.
- In a separate bowl, combine eggs, milk, and vanilla extract. Beat with a hand mixer until fluffy

- Now; add the wet ingredients to the bowl with dry ingredients. Mix until you get a thick batter. Add raspberries and stir with a spatula.
- Pour the mixture in silicone muffin molds and set aside
- Plug in the instant pot and pour 1 cup of water in the stainless steel insert. Set the trivet on the bottom and place molds on top
- Close the lid and adjust the steam release handle. Press the "MANUAL" button and set the timer for 30 minutes. Cook on "HIGH" pressure.
- Meanwhile, combine all topping ingredients in a mixing bowl. Beat with a mixer until all well combined and creamy, Set aside.
- When you hear the cooker's end signal, perform a quick pressure release and open the pot
- Carefully a
- wire rack and let it cool completely.
- Using a pipping bag, swirl the mixture over each muffin. Refrigerate for 15 minutes before serving

Nutrition:

- Calories - 193
- Fat - 14.7g
- Carbs - 4.2g
- Protein - 7.1g

INDIAN PUDDING

Serving: 5

Ingredients:

- 3 cups heated milk
- 2 Tbsp sucanat
- 2 Tbsp unsalted butter
- 1/2 cup dark molasses
- 1/2 cup cornmeal
- 1 pear, cored and peeled
- 1 Tbsp butter
- 7 oz package of caramels
- 1/4 cup apple juice
- 1/2 tsp cinnamon

Directions:

- Slice the apples and pears into wedges.
- In the slow cooker, combine the apple juice, butter, cinnamon, and caramels. Cover and cook for 1 hour on low, or until everything is melted. Mix well.
- Add the apple and pear wedges, then turn to coat in the mixture. Cover and cook for 1 hour on low, or until fruits are fork tender. Serve warm.

Nutrition:

- Calories - 277.2

Made in the USA
Las Vegas, NV
11 March 2025